THE KINGDOM OF GOD:

PREACHED BY JESUS…FORGOTTEN BY US

BY

WAYNE BARRETT

CHRISTLIFE PUBLICATIONS

ISBN: 0615652999
ISBN-13: 978-0615652993 (ChristLife Publications)

TABLE OF CONTENTS

PREFACE

Jesus Christ preached the kingdom of God. He taught us to pray for God's kingdom to come. He delivered parable after parable about those invited into the kingdom of God, found to be in the kingdom of God, or shut out from the kingdom of God. The apostles continued proclaiming the message of the kingdom of God. And for those who responded to their message, they knew first and foremost that in the name of Jesus Christ they had been both called and saved out of the kingdom of this world, which is judged and perishing, into the kingdom of God, which is eternal. They knew that there were only two kingdoms and that all people were citizens of one of those kingdoms.

Do we know the same thing? Do we truly believe in the kingdom of God, preached by Jesus Himself? Do we see this world in terms of the two kingdoms with our hearts set daily on seeking God's? Is this the defining and dominant concept of American Christianity?

Prosperous, compromised, and lovers of religious practice—that was the state of God's people to whom prophets such as Amos and Hosea were called to deliver scathing and graphic rebukes. And these were the people upon whom divine judgments were inflicted for their spiritual adultery. Can anyone deny that American Christianity is in the same jeopardy and for the same reasons? Pervasively, an understanding and proclamation of the most basic truths of why Jesus came and what is expected of Christians is critically lacking—and this in a culture of people who claim to very educated when it comes to the faith and who may be in church every Sunday.

This book is an effort to address, at least at a most basic level, some of the ignorance, neglect, and corruption concerning the kingdom of God that is prevalent in popular American Christianity. And it is an attempt to help equip willing Christians to function in God's kingdom in ways that He has provided. I certainly understand that there are count-less Christians in America who do not need such a challenge. We see them at work, in our communities, and in our congregations. We are constantly humbled and taught by their faithful lives and witness. You yourself may be just such an example. And yet, while I recognize that all Christians do not need to have their current model for Christian identity and living subjected to challenges, it is impossible to avoid what is obvious: many do. The American Church needs a renewal of the first order, one in which Christians truly repent, confess their sin, despise and cast off pride and pretense, die to self, and place all that they are and have at God's disposal. And the Church needs both to understand and to embrace the gospel of the kingdom of God.

So this book is written primarily for those who call themselves Christians. In particular, it is written to those who call themselves Christians in the United States of America, as it addresses a number of common shortcomings and failings of American Christianity. It is also written for anyone who desires to learn more about what it means to be a Christian.

My desire, and I hope it is yours as well, is that the life of Christ be manifested in His Church to His everlasting glory and praise. To that end, I hope that if you need it you are challenged, first, to examine yourself to be sure that you are in the faith. If you find that you do not have a faith relationship with Christ, I pray that you will accept His great invitation into His kingdom by repenting of your sin, being reconciled to God through Christ, and receiving the new life that He offers. If you do belong to Christ, and this book has relevance for you, I pray that God will use it according to His will and purposes to help you to grow in your understanding of what it means to enter and belong to His king-dom. May your life increasingly bring glory to Christ, may you be filled with His love and joy, and when you stand before Him, may He say that in your lifetime you ministered unto Him.

Wayne Barrett
Huntsville, Texas

What is the kingdom of God like? And to what shall I compare it?

—Luke 13:18

INTRODUCTION:
RE-WRITING THE SCRIPT

He who has ears to hear, let him hear.
—Matthew 11:15

Most of us believe that we are teachable. A person might even point to the fact that he is reading a book to indicate that he is. But in fact, many of us maintain a high resistance to any learning that would actually require a significant change in our behaviors or even in our outlooks. We don't mind learning new facts or having our emotions stirred or being given something to think about. But making a real change in our lives, including our true belief system…that's another matter. If you learn that there are twenty-seven books in the New Testament, that may be useful information, and you may be happy to know it, but it is unlikely that this knowledge is going to place any direct demands upon your living or beliefs. That's one reason you are happy to know it. On the other hand, if you learn that Jesus said "Love your enemies," or "Any one of you who does not renounce all that he has cannot be my disciple," you may be far less happy to know it. But pleased or not, the question of whether or not we are "teachable" is not answered by whether or not we know that Jesus said these things. We are teachable if we are willing, in spite of a storm of inner objections and excuse-making, to allow our lives to be changed by what we have learned—and by the One who has taught us.

And so it is good and important for one who says he is a disciple of Jesus Christ to ask himself once in a while, "Am I teachable?" Is it truly possible for me to learn something new and then to change or to allow changes to my way of thinking and my behavior based upon what I have learned? Or am I just so old, or so young, or so smart, or so ignorant, or so experienced, or so tired, or so busy, or so … that nothing I hear or read or observe is really going to make any difference in what I think and in what I do? Am I learning in order just to place more files into the cabinets of my knowledge, or am I learning how to live by living what I learn?

The reason Jesus preached was that we might both hear and respond. He taught in order for His followers to learn, to grow, to become increasingly useful to His work, to become more like Him, to increase in love for Him and for others, to experience His joy, and to be prepared by Him for an eternity which He has created and which is beyond our present comprehension.

For you to experience all that Jesus desires for us, you must be willing to accept His script for explaining and guiding your life. Not your script. His script. If a person is not willing to abandon his own script and allow it to be replaced by Jesus' script, then he is not really teachable. In that case, he is merely seeking affirmation or help for his own schemes. But if you are teachable, you have relinquished ownership of your script, and you now allow Jesus to write on your heart and in your mind those formulations and ideas that He desires you to have. You allow Him to direct your actions, to determine your habits, and to have ownership of your time. You have truly given your life to Jesus, you belong to Him, and that is a daily, ongoing, unqualified, and unending state of your life, no matter what your age, occupation, social position, aspirations, career, plans—no matter what. Complete surrender.

That is why Jesus is called Lord.

A chief problem—perhaps the chief problem—in the American Church today is that many professing Christians are not obedient to Christ, nor are they striving to be. But what compounds this tragic condition and what enables it is that they have convinced themselves that they are. They have a script, a pattern of ideas and habits, defining, to themselves, what it means to "be a Christian." And they follow that script. The more they follow their own script, the more they are convinced that they are living a life approved by God, when in fact they are living a life approved by themselves.

The script contains what they have placed there. It may involve going to church—and that, of course, will be to a church that "they like" and that "meets their needs" and has "good programs," especially for the kids! It may involve financial support (although it will not nearly as often involve sacrificial, i.e. truly costly, giving). It usually involves experiencing emotion during a "worship service," whether the emotion of excitement and adrenalin that some music may produce, or emotions of sympathy or remorse or sentiment, or emotions of motivation and confidence—the key is that some powerful emotional response is created, because that means it was a good service, or a good message, or great worship, or what have you. And that emotional experience fulfills its part of the script.

Their script may involve some very worthy activities: Bible reading, prayer, involvement in a ministry activity, some charitable actions—but it is still their script, not Christ's. They have ownership of the script. The script must meet their own approval. The script is the standard by which they evaluate Christian living. The more they invest themselves in their own script, the more convinced they are about it and the more difficult it becomes for them truly to learn something new—not because they are so "rebellious," but because they are so self-satisfied.

So are you really teachable? When you read the Bible, or hear a sermon, or read a Christian book, or, for that matter, when you are doing none of these things, is your script—your ideas and habits relating to what it means, in your opinion, to "be a Christian"—handed over to Christ to allow Him to make whatever changes or additions He desires? He might tear out some pages and throw them away. He might add some pages that you never would have added yourself. Are you willing to let Him do it? Are you willing to hear the voice of Christ and to be obedient without filtering that voice through your approval process and measuring it against the script you yourself have composed?

Sometimes our scripts seem to be very religious and for that reason we feel justified about clinging to them tenaciously. But remember that one can be very "religious" but not even know Christ. One can pray and read the Bible and not know Christ. The Pharisees were scrupulously religious and devout and yet they did not recognize the very person of

God Himself when He was speaking to them. Do you? And when you hear that voice, do you fall at His feet and place all of your life at His disposal—thoughts and actions and possessions and plans and time—or do you say "how nice" or "good message" or "interesting book" and keep right on, forever unchanged, in pursuing your own script of "Christian" living?

Have Thine own way, Lord! Have Thine own way!
Thou art the Potter; I am the clay.
                                    —Adelaide A. Pollard

THE KINGDOM OF THIS WORLD AND ITS RULER

Now is the judgment of this world; now will the ruler of this world be cast out.

—John 12:31

Why did Jesus come? There are many ways to answer this question correctly, and there are many ways to answer it incorrectly, but we are going to give attention to a particular answer—a perspective—that Jesus Himself consistently taught and that is echoed throughout the remainder of Scripture: *Jesus came to take back His kingdom.*

Jesus came to rescue His kingdom from the kingdom of the world, which is controlled by Satan. This one truth, if we really believe it, can change our lives and give direction to our living every day in every aspect. If we really believe it. The problem is that many do not believe it—even those who call themselves Christian. Or if they do believe it, it is only in some disconnected intellectual sense. For when they envision what it means to be a Christian, they never, and I do mean never, think of "being a Christian" in terms of belonging to and waiting for the kingdom of Christ which He is rescuing from the kingdom of this world, ruled by Satan. And yet this is exactly what Jesus taught, what the apostles taught, and what the early Christians understood.

Let us begin to look at this truth by looking at the part, in particular, that many professing Christians do not believe or may claim to believe but do not take seriously for a minute, and that is:

There is a kingdom of this world,
and the devil is the ruler of it.

At the very beginning of Jesus' public ministry, Matthew's gospel says that Jesus was "led up by the Spirit into the wilderness to be tempted by the devil."[1] The third and final temptation is recorded as follows:

> Again, the devil took him to a very high mountain and showed him all the kingdoms of the world and their glory. And he said to him, "All these I will give you, if you will fall down and worship me." Then Jesus said to him, "Be gone, Satan! For it is written, 'You shall worship the Lord your God and him only shall you serve.'"[2]

Already we see the elements of this great conflict into which Jesus entered. It is the devil, Satan, whom Jesus must now engage at the very beginning of His earthly ministry. The Apostle John was later to summarize the life and ministry of Jesus by saying that "the reason the Son of God appeared was to destroy the works of the devil."[3] And the devil, in this particular temptation, promises to give to Jesus "all the kingdoms of the world and their glory" if Jesus will worship him. Now although we know that the devil is a liar,[4] we must accept that his ability to deliver on this promise had some plausibility, or it would hardly have been a temptation at all—let alone his last and most desperate effort. And Jesus does not choose to challenge Satan's claim that he could deliver the kingdoms of this world, such as they are. Instead he rebukes Satan for seeking what only belongs to God, worship, the very thing that Satan desired and continues to desire.

Jesus often referred to the devil and his role in the world, both as its ruler and as the adversary. When Jesus explained the Parable of the Weeds to his disciples, He said "The one who sows the good seed is the Son of Man. The field is the world, and the good seed is the sons of the kingdom. The weeds are the sons of the evil one, and the enemy who sowed them is the devil."[5] In explaining the Parable of the Sower, Jesus said "The seed is the word of God. The ones along the path are those who have heard; then the devil comes and takes away the word from their hearts, so that they may not believe and be saved."[6] Much later, as Jesus' earthly ministry approached its conclusion, after His triumphal entry into Jerusalem and as Jesus knew that His crucifixion was imminent, He said: "Now is the judgment of this world; now will the *ruler of this world* be cast out."[7] As He spoke with His disciples to prepare them and reassure them, He said, "I will no longer talk much with you, for the *ruler of this world* is coming. He has no claim on me, but I do as the Father has commanded me, so that the world may know that I love the Father."[8] And as He taught His disciples about the coming and the ministry of the Holy Spirit, Jesus said that the Holy Spirit would convict the world "concerning judgment, because the *ruler of this world* is judged."[9] The writer of Hebrews tells us that "since therefore the children share in flesh and blood, he [Jesus] himself likewise partook of the same things, that through death he might destroy the one who has the power of death, that is, the devil."[10]

The Apostle Paul wrote to the church at Ephesus to "put on the whole armor of God, that you may be able to stand against the schemes of the devil. For we do not wrestle against flesh and blood, but against the rulers, against the authorities, against the cosmic powers over this present darkness, against the spiritual forces of evil in the heavenly places."[11] And to the church at Corinth he wrote that "then comes the end, when he [Jesus] delivers the kingdom to God the Father after destroying every rule and every authority and power."[12] We see the grand design, that Jesus came to rescue, to regain, His kingdom from the kingdom of the world and will present it to the Father. The apostle Peter warns us that "your adversary the devil prowls around like a roaring lion, seeking someone to devour."[13] And in the letter to the church at Smyrna, Jesus said "Do not fear what you are about to suffer. Behold, the devil is about to throw some of you into prison, that you may be tested, and for ten days you will have tribulation. Be faithful unto death, and I will give you the crown of life."[14]

As Satan's ultimate defeat is described in the book of Revelation, we read that "the great dragon was thrown down, that ancient serpent, who is called the devil and Satan, the deceiver of the whole world—he was thrown down to the earth, and his angels were thrown down with him."[15]

And throughout the New Testament we are taught that this world—the kingdom of this world—is separated from God, is under His judgment, and is at enmity with God. We are taught that the people of

Christ are being rescued out of the kingdom of the world into a different kingdom, the kingdom of Christ.

The High Priestly Prayer of Jesus is filled with references to this reality. "I have manifested your name to the people whom you gave me out of the world. Yours they were, and you gave them to me, and they have kept your word."[16] "I am praying for them. I am not praying for the world but for those whom you have given me, for they are yours."[17] "I have given them your word, and the world has hated them because they are not of the world, just as I am not of the world. I do not ask that you take them out of the world, but that you keep them from the evil one. They are not of the world, just as I am not of the world."[18] "O righteous Father, even though the world does not know you, I know you, and these know that you have sent me."[19]

When Paul preached in Ephesus, we are told that he "entered the synagogue and for three months spoke boldly, reasoning and persuading them about *the kingdom of God*"[20], and in his farewell to the Ephesians said "And now, behold, I know that none of you among whom I have gone about proclaiming *the kingdom* will see my face again."[21] When Paul was taken to Rome, for two years he "welcomed all who came to him, proclaiming *the kingdom of God* and teaching about the Lord Jesus Christ with all boldness."[22] Paul wrote to the Corinthians that "we have received not the *spirit of the world*, but the Spirit who is from God, that we might understand the things freely given us by God."[23] And later in the same letter wrote that "when we are judged by the Lord, we are disciplined so that we may not be condemned along with *the world*."[24] He cautioned the Colossians to "see to it that no one takes you captive by philosophy and empty deceit, according to human tradition, according to the elemental *spirits of the world*, and not according to Christ."[25] There is no question that as Paul preached and wrote, he did so within a framework of proclaiming the kingdom of God in contradistinction to the kingdom of this world.

James wrote "You adulterous people! Do you not know that friendship with the world is enmity with God? Therefore whoever wishes to be a friend of the world makes himself an enemy of God."[26] Peter wrote that in Christ we "may become partakers of the divine nature, having escaped from the corruption that is in the world because of sinful desire."[27]

John's letters are filled with contrasts made between the two kingdoms. He wrote "Do not love the world or the things in the world. If anyone loves the world, the love of the Father is not in him. For all that is in the world—the desires of the flesh and the desires of the eyes and pride in possessions—is not from the Father but is from the world. And the world is passing away along with its desires, but whoever does the will of God abides forever."[28] And later in the same letter: "Little children, you are from God and have overcome them, for he who is in you is greater than he who is in the world. They are from the world; therefore they speak from the world, and the world listens to them. We are from God. Whoever knows God listens to us; whoever is not from God does not listen to us. By this we know the Spirit of truth and the spirit of error."[29]

As the great and eternal triumph of Christ is announced in the book of Revelation, we read "The kingdom of the world has become the kingdom of our Lord and of his Christ, and he shall reign forever and ever."[30]

Now I do not know what it takes to convince you of something, but if you do not believe that there is a such a thing as a kingdom of the world and that the devil, Satan, is the ruler of that kingdom, then you simply do not believe what is taught in the Bible. You do not believe what Jesus taught and what the apostles taught and what is taught from the beginning of the New Testament to its very conclusion.

And if you do believe it, how often do you talk about it? How often does it even come into your mind? When you seek to understand what is going on in the world, whether on a global scale or in your hometown or in your workplace or in your own home, do you think in these terms—that the world is a fallen kingdom ruled by the devil—or do you think only in terms of politics, economics, family, commerce, social structures, nations, ethnicities, psychology, or any other of dozens of categories? Do you leave out entirely the all-encompassing category of the kingdom of the world and the devil, its ruler? Does that sound just too primitive or simple or silly or childish or old-fashioned or superstitious when compared to your much more sophisticated analyses? If so, just where did you get the idea that recognition of a spiritual being who is powerful enough to rule hearts and minds of men and the earth itself and who rules over other powerful spiritual beings, who manifests his will in the horrors and pain and suffering of humans that surround us every day, where did you get the idea that recognition of this being, whom Jesus Himself recognized, is childish or primitive or silly? You did not get it from the Bible, or from reason, or from experience.

This basic fact—there is a kingdom of the world whose ruler is the devil—is certainly not the only fact, or even the main fact that you need to understand as a Christian, but if you do not understand it and really believe it, you have a very incomplete notion of what is truly going on in this world—including in your personal life. The way you think about this truth of the two kingdoms, what you believe about it, will impact how you live every day and your constant state of mind.

Jesus came to take back His kingdom from the kingdom of the world, controlled by Satan. We have taken a look at what the Bible teaches broadly about the kingdom of the world. Let us begin to take a closer look at the kingdom of God.

All hail the power of Jesus' name!
 Let Angels prostrate fall:
Bring forth the royal diadem,
 To crown Him Lord of All.

Ye seed of Israel's chosen race,
 Ye ransomed of the fall,
Hail Him who saves you by his grace,
 And crown Him Lord of All.
      —Edward Perronet

The Kingdom of God: An Actual Kingdom

Repent, for the kingdom of heaven is at hand.
                                          —Matthew 3:2

Kingdom.

A word often creates images and stimulates associations in our mind, and those impressions, made by the same word, vary considerably among people. This is certainly true of the word *kingdom*. For this reason, let's give some attention to the word *kingdom* before we go any further with its discussion.

For those in Jesus' day, a kingdom was a living, present reality—a form of government with which all of his listeners were quite familiar. They knew exactly what a kingdom was and did not have to think too much about it.

Today, we may know that a kingdom is a realm ruled by a monarch, a sovereign ruler, who essentially answers to no one, whose word and power is unquestioned, and who has complete authority over every person and every thing. But even though we know it intellectually, we do not understand a kingdom in the same deep, existential way as does someone who has actually lived in a kingdom as a subject to a king.

Those who live in today's monarchies that also have parliamentary representation may feel that they do have an understanding of a kingdom, but the representative system under which they are governed is a far cry from a kingdom in the older and unmodified sense of the word. Closer to understanding a kingdom may be those persons who have lived, or do live, under totalitarian governments with a dictator and ruling political party of some sort. They understand indeed what it is like to be governed without any regard whatsoever to what they believe or desire, i.e. what it is to be *ruled*. And while it does not follow that all kings are evil dictators or party chairmen, it does follow that kings rule and subjects obey.

Those who have grown up under democratically-based governments, republics in which individuals have secured rights under law and in which the rights of individuals are continually being asserted and discovered, may have a great deal of difficulty adapting to the idea of a kingdom, no matter how much lip service they may give. It is challenging indeed for these citizens, as they think of government and authority, to conceive of an arrangement in which their opinion or permission is not sought or even significant and in which no question ever has to be put up for a vote. A system in which the ruler rules, and in which his decisions do not need to conform to any pre-established, legal agreements. The ruler answers only to himself. They might consider such a condition to be slavery. But while slavery is unacceptable in terms of human politics and governments, the idea of it is not entirely inaccurate or unacceptable when considering what it is to live in a kingdom.[31] So if the idea of slavery helps some who live in democratically-based governments to understand what it is to be in a kingdom, although slavery is not exactly the same thing, they might use the analogy.

It may be important here to point out that all concepts of sovereign authority should not be negative: there are and have been good kings, just as there are good employers, and good fathers. What is a foreign concept to many of us moderns, however, is the model of *any* type, good or bad, of an absolute ruler, and unfortunately, most, if not all, of our modern examples of that are negative ones.[32] We may have to resort to utilizing history or even our imagination to recognize that an absolute ruler's authority can be a good thing—depending upon the ruler.

And in this regard, if we only focus on the authority of the monarch and little else, we are thinking of kingdoms in a very limited and skewed way. Kingdoms *belong* to the monarch, and his subjects are able to live by enjoying resources that are not theirs—they are the crown's. So kings—good ones—provide blessings and protection to those who otherwise would not have it. Under the rule of a benevolent monarch, the subjects of the king enjoy gifts and opportunities for life that are made possible by the king. In such a kingdom, the king's authority hardly has to be imposed by force as great loyalty and thankfulness will exist among the subjects. "Long live the King!" becomes their sincere and enthusiastic expression. And those who are punished by a good king's authority in such a kingdom are deserving evildoers who not only have rebelled against the crown, but have corrupted and harmed his kingdom. The punishment of evildoers is actually good and necessary for the kingdom, protecting the faithful and true subjects and maintaining the lives that they enjoy.

The kingdom of God, or the kingdom of Heaven (both terms are used in the New Testament) is the realm of God. He is the Creator, He owns it, He sustains it, He gives life and light and energy and joy to all its citizens, and He rules it in inexpressible love and glory and power. The kingdom of God is both spiritual and material, just as we are. It is a kingdom of love and laughter and affection and joy and excitement and peace, and it is a kingdom of the One who created hummingbirds, waterfalls, galaxies, mountains, flowers, smells, sounds, taste, touch, and sight. It is a kingdom of intellect and reason, of creaturely rest and repose, a kingdom without violence, without envy, without selfishness, without pain, without illness. It is a kingdom where God is worshiped and adored and in which God Himself is all in all.[33]

God's kingdom is real. It is not just an idea or a metaphor. It is a actual and eternal realm to which a person does or does not have admittance. It is not a "belief" or a matter of opinion or a state of mind. Jesus preached that all should "repent, for the kingdom of heaven is at hand."[34] He taught that our priority for living should be to "seek first His [God's] kingdom and His righteousness."[35] He also warned with emphasis that "unless you are converted and become like children, you will not enter the kingdom of heaven."[36] In describing the fate of those who would not be saved, He said:

> When once the master of the house has risen and shut the door, and you begin to stand outside and to knock at the door, saying, 'Lord, open to us,' then he will answer you, 'I do not know where you come from.' Then you

will begin to say, 'We ate and drank in your presence, and you taught in our streets.' But he will say, 'I tell you, I do not know where you come from. Depart from me, all you workers of evil!' In that place there will be weeping and gnashing of teeth, when you see Abraham and Isaac and Jacob and all the prophets in the kingdom of God but you yourselves cast out. And people will come from east and west, and from north and south, and recline at table in the kingdom of God.[37]

The kingdom of God should be the prayer, the desire, the hope, the ever-present reality for those who are followers of Christ. Jesus preached and taught constantly on the kingdom of God. He gave parable after parable about His kingdom. He called and invited. He described. He warned. The gospel Jesus preached was the gospel of the kingdom, and that was the gospel that His apostles preached. And that is the gospel that we must believe, and preach, and understand.

Where is God's kingdom? Is it present now, or is it something we are waiting for? Who is in God's kingdom, and who is not? These are the subjects of the next chapters.

We've a Savior to show to the nations
Who the path of sorrow hath trod,
That all of the world's great peoples
Might come to the truth of God.

For the darkness shall turn to dawning,
And the dawning to noon-day bright,
And Christ's great kingdom shall come on earth,
The kingdom of love and light.
                              —E. Ernest Nichol

THE KINGDOM OF GOD:
WHO IS EXCLUDED?

For many are called, but few are chosen.
—Matthew 22:14

God's kingdom is not open to entry based simply upon one's choice.[38] No one merely gets to decide that he will become a citizen of God's kingdom. That would be like "deciding" that someone will leave you an inheritance, or that someone will give you a gift, or that you can move into someone else's house—except that the idea that we can just "decide" to enter God's kingdom is infinitely more preposterous than any of these analogies .

Entry into God's kingdom is by invitation only—His invitation. Jesus came to issue that invitation and to secure the means by which we can respond to it. It is through Jesus Christ, and only through Him, that we are able to become children of God and gain admittance into God's kingdom. In short, those who gain entry into God's kingdom are those, and only those, whom God has invited and chosen. These are often referred to in the New Testament as the "elect," meaning, elected by God.

This invitation of God through Christ, man's individual responses to that invitation, and the consequences of those responses constitute the overarching theme of the Bible: God's redemption—i.e. His buying back—of a people who are separated from Him because of sin. There is no better summary of this theme than that found in the often-quoted John 3:16: "For God so loved the world, that he gave his only Son, that whoever believes in him should not perish but have eternal life." From the beginning of the preaching of Jesus, to the descriptions of the end of history in the book of Revelation, God's saving work in Christ is the theme. In his letter to the church in Corinth, Paul summarizes this theme by saying that

> in Christ God was reconciling the world to himself, not counting their trespasses against them, and entrusting to us the message of reconciliation. Therefore, we are ambassadors for Christ, God making his appeal through us. We implore you on behalf of Christ, be reconciled to God.[39]

God invites. God, in His great love, has done what is necessary, through Jesus Christ, His Son, to pay the debt that our sins have caused. Jesus said "Come to me, all who labor and are heavy laden, and I will give you rest."[40] The preaching of the apostles was that men should come and be reconciled to God. And in the very last chapter of Scripture, as the book of Revelation and the New Testament come to a close, we read

> The Spirit and the Bride [the Church] say, "Come." And let the one who hears say, "Come." And let the one who is thirsty come; let the one who desires take the water of life without price.[41]

God has made this sacrifice and issued His invitation because it is His great and earnest desire that we should return to Him. The Apostle Peter tells us that God "is patient toward you, not wishing that any should perish, but that all should reach repentance."[42] Jesus said "Fear not, little flock, for it is your Father's good pleasure to give you the kingdom."[43] And we are repeatedly made to understand that Jesus came to save the world—all who believe in Him and follow Him. Just before He ascended to heaven after His resurrection, Jesus charged His disciples to make disciples of all peoples. And He told them that they would be His witnesses to the uttermost parts of the earth. God's invitation is to all who will respond in faith.

Not all who hear God's call, however, respond in a way that results in their being saved; they do not enter God's kingdom. Some delay with excuses and then find that subsequent opportunities to respond do not present themselves. Others refuse outright. Others respond initially in a positive way to God's call but later, when their faith is challenged or becomes costly, they abandon and deny Christ.

It would be incorrect to consider the costly and undeserved invitation of God to be some sort of "standing offer" to which a person can choose to respond whenever he decides that he is ready. Quite the contrary. Based upon the teachings of Jesus and the apostles, it would be better (though not entirely accurate) to think of God's invitation as a "one-time offer" than as a "standing offer," if you had to think of it as one way or the other. Jesus told numerous parables that revealed a low tolerance for those who receive an invitation to God's kingdom but respond with excuses or for those who respond to the invitation in a way that shows disrespect or carelessness. To support this with scriptural references would constitute an entire book in itself. One representative passage is from Luke 9:

> To another he [Jesus] said, "Follow me." But he said, "Lord, let me first go and bury my father." And Jesus said to him, "Leave the dead to bury their own dead. But as for you, go and proclaim the kingdom of God." Yet another said, "I will follow you, Lord, but let me first say farewell to those at my home." Jesus said to him, "No one who puts his hand to the plow and looks back is fit for the kingdom of God."

And while we are not told that these persons never had another opportunity to respond to the call of Jesus, such opportunities are not recorded in Scripture. We certainly do not see Jesus endlessly and repetitively seeking out persons who have turned away from His call and asking them to reconsider. We never see Him doing that. And we are warned over and over not to harden our hearts and resist the invitation of God, thus presuming upon God's patience. The writer of Hebrews warned:

> Take care, brothers, lest there be in any of you an evil, unbelieving heart, leading you to fall away from the living God. But exhort one another every day, as long as it is called "today," that none of you may be hardened by the deceitfulness of sin. For we have come to share in Christ, if indeed we hold our original confidence firm to the end. As it is said, "Today, if you hear his voice, do not harden your hearts as in the rebellion."[44]

How long does a person have to respond to God's invitation? That is up to God. And it is God's desire that those who are called respond in faith and obedience. Jesus came that "whoever believes in Him might not perish." But it is not Biblical or sound or safe to think that the door of opportunity to respond to God's invitation will remain open throughout one's life no matter what one does, no matter how one responds. It is perilous and foolish to resist and refuse God's invitation, and we are warned not to do it.

For those who choose to refuse God's call outright, those who reject Christ, the outcome is a bad one, almost too terrible to contemplate, and on this point the teaching of Jesus and the apostles is completely consistent and clear. Those persons die in their sins, they die as unrepentant citizens of the kingdom of this world, and, since they have rejected the only provision that exists and that can exist for the forgiveness of their sins, they are consigned forever in a place of eternal punishment. Jesus taught us that His word to them will be "Depart from me, you cursed, into the eternal fire prepared for the devil and his angels."[45] Jesus also said "whoever denies me before men, I also will deny before my Father who is in heaven.[46] On another occasion, when Jesus was emphasizing how strongly someone should seek to live according to God's will, He said "if your eye causes you to sin, tear it out. It is better for you to enter the kingdom of God with one eye than with two eyes to be thrown into hell, 'where their worm does not die and the fire is not quenched.'"[47] In Paul's letter to Timothy, he wrote that "if we deny him [Jesus], he also will deny us;"[48] And at the very end of the Bible, we read that if anyone's name was not found written in the book of life, he was thrown into the lake of fire."[49]

These citation do not even come close to being all of the passages in the New Testament that concern the fate of those who have rejected Jesus Christ. It is reinforced over and over again. The fact that many churches have ceased to teach this dominant and unavoidable major theme of Scripture does not make it any less true. The fact that many persons today consider such warnings to be just oh so much superstitious nonsense does not make it any less true. There is a judgment that awaits every person. Those whose names are not found in Jesus' book of life, those who have rejected Him, will be judged and sentenced to eternal fire.

It is also necessary for those who have placed their faith in Christ to persevere until the end. There are those who hear the word of Christ, whether in childhood or adulthood, and when they hear it, they gladly accept it and they begin to follow Christ in a happy but superficial understanding and commitment. There is little depth to their faith. As they go forward, and as they begin to encounter the challenges and perplexities that come to those who follow Christ, they are not willing to meet those challenges, and they walk away from Him. They reject Jesus and His kingdom for the sake of the world. Jesus described such a person as "one who hears the word and immediately receives it with joy, yet he has no root in himself, but endures for a while, and when tribulation or persecution arises on account of the word, immediately he falls away."[50] We have already seen that Jesus said "No one who puts his hand to the plow and looks back is fit for the kingdom of God."[51] He also said to the believers in the church at Smyrna "Do not fear what you are about to suffer. Behold, the devil is about to throw some of you into prison, that you may be tested, ... *Be faithful unto death*, and I will give you the crown of life."[52] Jesus made it clear that those who would belong to His kingdom must persevere, life's challenges notwithstanding—and some of those challenges may be severe ones.

Jesus also made it clear, and the rest of Scripture reinforces this abundantly, that it is He, Jesus Himself, who keeps us and who gives us the strength to persevere. He is our shepherd. He is with us always, even to the close of the age. He guards us. He protects us. He prays for us. He has sent the Holy Spirit to dwell in believers who changes us, empowers us, prays for us, teaches us, encourages us, and is the seal, the promise, the guarantee of our inheritance in Christ. Jesus forgives our sin. He bears with us in our weakness. He is merciful and loving. He carries us in His arms when our faith has been exhausted. It is God who is at work within us, both to will and to work for His good pleasure.

It remains, however, that some persons begin, or certainly seem to begin, a life of following Christ. They may begin with great enthusiasm. But when troubles come, they do not turn to Christ for help in their weakness, they turn away from Him and go back to the world. They change their minds. They reject and deny their Savior. And consequently they have no place in the kingdom of God.

Jesus sustains us in our weakness, even when we run out of faith, and He does not cast us away because we sin. But those who deny Jesus will be denied by Him. Nowhere are these truths summarized more succinctly than in what may have been an early Christian hymn, or part of one, that Paul includes in a letter to Timothy:

> If we have died with him, we will also live with him;
> if we endure, we will also reign with him;
> if we deny him, he also will deny us;
> if we are faithless, he remains faithful—for he cannot deny himself.[53]

There are two kingdoms, the kingdom of the world and the kingdom of God. Every person is associated with one or the other. There are no exemptions, and there is no middle ground. God invites all who will respond to be reconciled to Him and return to His loving care.

We have looked with a little detail at those who will not enter His kingdom. Let us look now at those who do.

When the trumpet of the Lord shall sound, and time shall be no more,
  And the morning breaks, eternal, bright and fair;
When the saved of earth shall gather over on the other shore,
  And the roll is called up yonder, I'll be there.
                                    —James M. Black

THE KINGDOM OF GOD: WHO IS ADMITTED?

"Truly, truly, I say to you, unless one is born again he cannot see the kingdom of God."

—John 3:3

Those who belong to God's kingdom are those who have become children of God through repentance of their sin and faith in Jesus Christ.

We gain entry to God's kingdom through the work of Jesus Christ on our behalf. It is a gift of God's great love. "For God so loved the world that He gave His only Son." We cannot earn it, just as no gift, by definition, is earned. But in this case, not only is the gift not earned, it is completely undeserved. There is nothing about us that would even begin to deserve such a gift of God. What we actually deserve is punishment, because we have all sinned against God. So God's gift of love in Christ is a gift of grace.

God invites us to His banquet, or we could not come. He opens our minds and hearts to hear and understand His message, or we could not respond. And the way that we are to respond is that we place our faith in Christ. "He [Jesus] came to his own, and his own people did not receive him. But to all who did receive him, who believed in his name, he gave the right to become children of God."[54] Jesus came "that whoever believes in Him should not perish but have eternal life."[55] And Jesus said "I am the way, and the truth, and the life. No one comes to the Father except through me."[56] The call to faith in Jesus Christ is the theme of the New Testament and to cite all supporting scriptures would necessitate writing almost all of it.

Jesus calls those who are brought into God's kingdom His Church. This word, church, is a translation of the Greek word *ekklesia*, which means "called out ones." The people of God, His people, His Church, are a separated people, God's Kingdom, who are *in* this world but who are not longer *of* this world. As previously mentioned, Jesus prayed to the Father for His disciples:

> I have given them your word, and the world has hated them because they are not of the world, just as I am not of the world. I do not ask that you take them out of the world, but that you keep them from the evil one. They are not of the world, just as I am not of the world.[57]

Jesus taught very early on in His ministry that God's people are the "light of the world"[58] and the "salt of the earth."[59] The Church manifests His very presence in the world. And the Church belongs to Him so intimately and exclusively that in Scripture it is called the Bride of Christ.

Those who were members of the Church were not identified as such because of some type of institutional affiliation—including participation in organized religious events. Jesus and the Apostles taught that every person who truly places his faith in Christ is changed. Not reformed or improved. Re-created. Given a new life, a life that he did not have before, the very life of Christ. Jesus called it being "born again." Paul wrote that "if anyone is in Christ, he is a new creation. The old has passed away; behold, the new has come."[60] We receive this new birth by faith through the gift of the Holy Spirit—we must be born "of the Spirit." Paul said in his letter to the church in Rome "You, however, are not in the flesh but in the Spirit, if in fact the Spirit of God dwells in you. Anyone who does not have the Spirit of Christ does not belong to him."[61] This new birth, this new life, is the defining result of placing faith in Christ.

The early Christians were not vague upon this point at all. Receiving the Holy Spirit was the assurance each person had of his salvation. And it was having the life of the Spirit that was normally cited as the undeniable evidence that a person was in Christ. Paul wrote to the Christians in Galatia, who were abandoning faith for a legalistic approach to living, "Let me ask you only this: Did you receive the Spirit by works of the law or by hearing with faith? Are you so foolish? Having begun by the Spirit, are you now being perfected by the flesh?"[62] We recall that Paul wrote to the Romans "You, however, are not in the flesh but in the Spirit, if in fact the Spirit of God dwells in you. Anyone who does not have the Spirit of Christ does not belong to him."[63] When Paul came to Ephesus, he found some disciples there whom he asked "Did you receive the Holy Spirit when you believed?" And they said, "No, we have not even heard that there is a Holy Spirit."[64] Paul proceeded to teach them, baptize them in the name of Jesus, and laid his hands on them, at which time they received the Holy Spirit. Later, in Paul's letter to the church at Ephesus, he wrote "In him [Christ] you also, when you heard the word of truth, the gospel of your salvation, and believed in him, were sealed with the promised Holy Spirit, who is the guarantee of our inheritance until we acquire possession of it, to the praise of his glory."[65] For the early Church, the active, present, life of the Holy Spirit within believers was God's seal, sign, and assurance of their belonging to Him. And God has not changed.

But much of the church has. Today's tests and assurances of salvation often consist chiefly of asking whether or not someone agrees with certain statements of beliefs and may include a requirement that he associate with a particular congregation or denomination in the manner that is prescribed by them. What a contrast! And this mistake is compounded by the fact that professed believers in Christ feel that they can measure the depth and quality of their commitment to Him by professing to believe more and more statements. They feel particularly committed and notable when they can identify some statements they claim to believe that distinguish them from others who do not share their viewpoints. And these various professions of belief can occur, and with straight faces, with almost no regard whatsoever as to how a person is actually living, what his character is, and definitely without regard as to the manifest presence of the Holy Spirit in his life.

Let's look at this a little more closely so that there can be no confusion about it. Believing things about God is not enough, and believing more and more statements about God is still not enough. James made this point clear when he wrote "You believe that God is one; you do well. Even the demons believe—and shudder!"[66] We can expand on that thought. What if a person says, "I don't just believe in God, I believe that Jesus is the only-begotten Son of God."? Well, so does the devil—in fact, he knows it very well. "Well, I believe that Jesus died for my sins." So does the devil—he knows that Jesus died for your sins. "Well I believe that Jesus rose again, ascended into heaven, and sits and the right hand of the Father." So does the devil. "I believe that the Bible is the inspired, [fill in your own superlative adjectives here] word of God." So does the devil. In fact, he may tremble more at the word of God than you do. And you can go right on saying what you believe about God, Jesus, the Holy Spirit, the Bible, the communion of the saints, judgment, the resurrection of the dead, the second coming of Christ, and on and on and on, and as long as your statements are accurate, you have not said or done anything yet that distinguishes you from the devil, because he knows all those things to be true.

So what does distinguish a Christian from the devil? A Christian has become a child of God through repentance of his sin and faith in Christ. The differences with the devil are immediate. First of all, the devil has not repented of his sin and placed faith in Christ to save him. There's a difference. A Christian can say "I love Jesus". The devil cannot and will not say that. The Christian loves others with the very love of God. The devil loves no one. A Christian has been given the Holy Spirit. The devil most certainly has not. Consequently, a Christian's life begins to be characterized by qualities the Bible calls the fruit of the Spirit: love, joy, peace, patience, kindness, goodness, faithfulness, gentleness, and self-control.[67] The devil has none of those qualities, although he counterfeits them. A Christian performs acts of servanthood and sacrifice, acts of love and kindness and mercy, because those actions flow from the life of Christ that has been given to him. The devil's actions, all of them, are motivated by hate and self-will with self-glorification as their aim.

Does this mean that Christian creeds and doctrines are worthless? Certainly not. Many of the Scriptures are given to teach us what we should believe about certain realities, such as Christ's death on the cross, His resurrection, His second coming, and much, much more. If we are to grow into maturity as followers of Christ, if we are to make some sense of the world around us, if we desire to function effectively in relation-ships, if we desire guidance for decisions and insight for communications with others, for these and many more reasons what we know and profess is important. We are to "grow in the grace *and knowledge* of our Lord and Savior Jesus Christ."[68] But what must always be clear in our minds is that "being a Christian" does not mean that we merely affirm various facts—even spiritual facts—that the devil and his demons know as well as we do. The reason that creeds and truths have importance and power in our lives is that we affirm and proclaim these facts *from the standpoint of a faith relationship with Christ*: as those who have surrendered their lives to Jesus Christ, who are saved and given life by Him, who praise Him and long for His glory, who have received forgiveness and forgive others—from the standpoint of a people who have been called, chosen, filled with God's Spirit, and who belong exclusively to Him. Anyone can agree with a creed or quote the Bible. Only those who belong to God and who have been given new life by God can love Him with an everlasting love and reveal the character of God through their living.

A person is not saved by his works. A person is saved because he repents and places his faith in Christ to forgive him. The thief on the cross next to Jesus who was repentant and asked Jesus to "remember him" was forgiven and saved by Jesus at that moment.[69] That dying thief did not have a chance to go back and apologize to people he had wronged or return what he had stolen or live a life of good deeds or be baptized or take communion. He was saved because he was repentant, he recognized that Jesus was the Son of God, and he asked Jesus to save him. His salvation was a free gift in response to that faith—and that is the way salvation is given to anyone who has ever been saved or ever will be saved. A free gift of God in Christ. But had that thief continued to live on this earth, he would have been a different person indeed from the one who was sent to the cross. He was given a new life in Christ. He was changed. He was born again. And the change that accompanies salvation would have been evident to all who knew him.

So, those who are saved are saved by a gift from God. And that gift accompanies a new birth, spiritual birth, the receiving of the very life of

Christ, and it is this life in action that actually reveals that a person belongs to Christ. Jesus said "Truly, truly, I say to you, unless one is born again he cannot see the kingdom of God,"[70] and Jesus has not changed His mind or His message.

Amazing grace! (how sweet the sound!)
That saved a wretch like me!
I once was lost, but now am found;
Was blind, but now I see.

Through many dangers, toils, and snares,
I have already come;
'Tis grace hath brought me safe thus far,
And grace will lead me home.
                              —John Newton

THE KINGDOM OF GOD AS A FUTURE REALITY

Thy kingdom come.
                —Matthew 6:10

The Bible teaches several different perspectives on the kingdom of Heaven. All of them are true, and if a person sincerely believes them, it will greatly affect how he lives.

One perspective is that the kingdom of God is a new government of all creation that will be instituted on earth one day in the future when Christ comes again, replacing the present kingdom of the world, ruled by the devil. Many Christian teachings down through the years involve a good deal of elaboration on how all this will take place, and, in fact, the Bible speaks with much detail to this topic, both with great clarity and with great mystery.

Surprisingly, in the midst of all of the various teachings about apocalyptic events, including the Great Tribulation, the removal of the Church from the earth,[71] God's wrath, and the millennial reign of Christ, the power and hope and magnificence of the main message that God's eternal kingdom is coming has sometimes gotten lost in the details of eschatologies. It is sad but safe to say that the average Christian in the United States today gives very little thought on a daily or weekly or monthly or, dare we say, yearly, basis about the certain coming of God's kingdom and Christ's eternal reign. For so many Christians, tragically, this great hope may as well be so much talk. It is lost on them that they have been promised this magnificent eternal kingdom, that Jesus died so that they might be brought back into this kingdom, and that they now have been brought by the work and gift of Christ "to Mount Zion and to the city of the living God, the heavenly Jerusalem, and to innumerable angels in festal gathering, and to the assembly of the firstborn who are enrolled in heaven, and to God, the judge of all, and to the spirits of the righteous made perfect, and to Jesus, the mediator of a new covenant."[72] They are not encouraged by this, they are not enlivened by it, they do not look forward to this inheritance with longing and with wonder. When they pray "Thy kingdom come" their hearts do not stir at all with the certain hope that they have an eternal place in that kingdom. They have more anticipation of a weekend trip than they do the coming of Christ's kingdom. They have no vision of it. They do not picture it or imagine it. They do not talk about it, not among themselves and not among those who do not know about Christ. They never look into the sky and envision Jesus coming upon the clouds or the sky being rolled up like a scroll.[73] They are practically dead to this truth, and the reason they are dead to it is they do not believe it. They do not deny it, mind you, but they do not believe it, truly believe it in their hearts. If they did, every day would be informed and blessed and changed by this certain expectation.

God's kingdom is coming. This is certain. And when His kingdom comes, there will only be two reactions.

There will be those who welcome their Savior, who rejoice in the appearance of Jesus Christ, who fall on their faces in adoration and love and worship, and who are filled with inexpressible joy and wonder. When the Apostle Paul was facing his own death, and looking forward to that great day of Christ's appearing, he wrote "Henceforth there is laid up for me the crown of righteousness, which the Lord, the righteous judge, will award to me on that Day, and not only to me but also to all who have loved his appearing."[74] All those who belong to Christ will be those "who have loved his appearing."

For those who have rejected Christ, the reaction will be one of horror and despair. Having rejected the gracious provision made for their sin, they must now pay in full when, as Paul wrote to the church in Thessalonians,

> the Lord Jesus is revealed from heaven with his mighty angels in flaming fire, inflicting vengeance on those who do not know God and on those who

do not obey the gospel of our Lord Jesus. They will suffer the punishment of eternal destruction, away from the presence of the Lord and from the glory of his might, when he comes on that day to be glorified in his saints, and to be marveled at among all who have believed.[75]

When Jesus comes again, there will be a great judgment. And to those who belong to Him, He will say "Come, you who are blessed by my Father, inherit the kingdom prepared for you from the foundation of the world."[76] And to those who do not belong to Him, He will say "Depart from me, you cursed, into the eternal fire prepared for the devil and his angels."[77] Jesus Himself summarized this judgment by saying "These will go away into eternal punishment, but the righteous into eternal life."[78]

Following this judgment, God will destroy the heavens and the earth and replace them with a new heaven and a new earth. The Apostle Peter wrote that

> the day of the Lord will come like a thief, and then the heavens will pass away with a roar, and the heavenly bodies will be burned up and dissolved, and the earth and the works that are done on it will be exposed. Since all these things are thus to be dissolved, what sort of people ought you to be in lives of holiness and godliness, waiting for and hastening the coming of the day of God, because of which the heavens will be set on fire and dissolved, and the heavenly bodies will melt as they burn! But according to his promise we are waiting for new heavens and a new earth in which righteousness dwells.[79]

John saw this when he was given the revelation and wrote "Then I saw a new heaven and a new earth, for the first heaven and the first earth had passed away, and the sea was no more."[80] He goes on to describe this event:

> And I heard a loud voice from the throne saying, "Behold, the dwelling place of God is with man. He will dwell with them, and they will be his people, and God himself will be with them as their God. He will wipe away every tear from their eyes, and death shall be no more, neither shall there be mourning, nor crying, nor pain anymore, for the former things have passed away."[81]

What a place! What a kingdom! And this is the inheritance of all who belong to Jesus—indeed, our receiving this inheritance, this eternal life, in a place where all pain and sin is banished and where God reigns, was the very reason Jesus came, the very thing he died to give us, and the very future that He Himself has secured for us and promised us.

The kingdom of God is coming. It means eternal love and eternal joy for those who have received the gift of God in Christ, and it means an eternal sentence almost too horrible to contemplate, but too horrible *not* to contemplate, for those who have rejected their only means of salvation. Jesus Himself said to John

> It is done! I am the Alpha and the Omega, the beginning and the end. To the thirsty I will give from the spring of the water of life without payment. The one who conquers will have this heritage, and I will be his God and he will be my son. But as for the cowardly, the faithless, the detestable, as for murderers, the sexually immoral, sorcerers, idolaters, and all liars, their portion will be in the lake that burns with fire and sulfur, which is the second death.[82]

The person who believes this cannot live in an ordinary way. That person cannot walk and talk and plan and prioritize and interpret events and commit resources or make any assessment outside of and uninfluenced by this great truth and certainty of the coming of God's kingdom. And a person who understands that all people have an eternal destination, that all people are under God's judgment of sin, and that in Jesus Christ "there is salvation in no one else, for there is no other name under heaven given among men by which we must be saved"[83]—that person cannot simply allow the world around him to perish into eternal death without seeking to do all that God has called and equipped him to do in the name of Christ to rescue those who are lost and to build up the Church.

Do you believe that the kingdom of God is coming? Do you truly believe?

And Lord haste the day, when my faith shall be sight,
The clouds be rolled back as a scroll;
The trump shall resound, and the Lord shall descend,
Even so, it is well with my soul.
                              —Horatio Spafford

THE KINGDOM OF GOD AS A PRESENT REALITY

The kingdom of God is in your midst.
                                    —Luke 17:21

The kingdom of God is coming. A war is being waged in which those who belong to Christ are being called out of the kingdom of this world, are transformed by the power of Christ, and will inherit the kingdom prepared for them from the foundation of the world.

But Jesus and the Apostles also spoke of the kingdom of God as a present reality. Consider the following encounter of Jesus and some Pharisees:

> Being asked by the Pharisees when the kingdom of God would come, he answered them, "The kingdom of God is not coming in ways that can be observed, nor will they say, 'Look, here it is!' or 'There!' for behold, the kingdom of God is in the midst of you."[84]

The Apostle Paul wrote to the Romans "For the kingdom of God is not a matter of eating and drinking but of righteousness and peace and joy in the Holy Spirit.'[85] And he wrote to the Church in Corinth "For the kingdom of God does not consist in talk but in power."[86]

In each of these cases, the kingdom of God is described as something that is both present and internal. It is *in the midst of you*, it is *peace and joy in the Holy Spirit*, it is not talk but *power*. This is another perspective on the same reality—the reality of the kingdom of God—that we have been considering.

But how can it be the same reality? Because in these cases, it is the present spiritual condition of the hearers and questioners that is being addressed. A very serious error, a dangerous mindset, was prevalent

37

among some "religious" people during Christ's earthly ministry, continued during the days of the early church, and persists right up until the present time—certainly with great strength in the United States. That error is the belief or the mindset that God's kingdom is something that one can wait for or inherit or be a part of without true repentance, true faith, and new birth in Christ. And this mindset of satisfied self-righteousness is almost impenetrable. If we look at the teachings of Jesus and Paul that occur at the beginning of this chapter we will see that, in each case, it is this condition that was being confronted.

In the first case, the Pharisees where asking Jesus *when the kingdom of God would come*. The Pharisees asking Jesus this question did not have a faith relationship with Jesus. They had not repented. They did not acknowledge Him as the Lord of their lives. What they did have was a theology of their own about the Christ.[87] They had their own ideas about what the Christ was going to do when he arrived, based upon their interpretations of Scripture. And Jesus of Nazareth did not comport with their Messianic views. They were testing Jesus, testing His knowledge of their theology (which they would have defined as His knowledge of the Scriptures), and looking for ways to discredit or trap Him. The furthest thing from their religious minds was that they needed to make any change at all to belong to God's kingdom. They were already the devout! Others looked to them as the very epitome of religious dedication. Jesus pointed them away from their incomplete Messianic theology and their dead legalism to the fact that entrance into God's kingdom was occurring, unnoticed or disregarded, all around them. His message to them then was the same as when He began to preach, "Repent, for the kingdom of God is at hand."

In Paul's letter to the Romans, the Apostle was confronting a situation in which some people in the church, characterized by a judgmental, legalistic theology, were abusing others over their religious opinions—others whom Paul describes as weaker in faith.[88] The abusers had decided that their own opinions were of supreme importance. Paul reminds those who had begun to value their own opinions above all else, including love to a brother, that the true kingdom of God has no place for mistreating others, that God's kingdom is peace and joy in the Holy

Spirit. Paul goes on to say that "Whoever thus serves Christ," even if he does not share all of your views, "is acceptable to God and approved by men. So then let us pursue what makes for peace and for mutual upbuilding."[89]

In the third instance, where Paul was writing to the Corinthians, there were some great troublemakers in the church. They were dividing the church into camps and were teaching both doctrines and lifestyles that are antithetical to the Gospel of Jesus Christ. In order to do this with success, it was necessary to discredit the Apostle Paul and by extension his teachings, which they sought constantly to do. Paul was living far away and not there to defend himself, but he had heard about the problems and confronted these persons strongly in his letter. He reminds them that the kingdom of God does not consist in talk, in particular *their* talk, but in power—the power of God which was present in the life and teaching of Paul and which would prevail when he next visited the church. So in this case as well, there were persons, claiming to belong to the kingdom of God, but whose behavior did not support that assertion. And these were people who were assuming roles of leadership and influence in the church at Corinth. Paul addresses their spiritual condition which places them outside the kingdom of God and ignorant of its true nature.

The kingdom of God is the realm where God reigns, and His reign begins with the lives of those who belong to His kingdom. That reign in our lives has already been initiated, and so for all who will inherit God's kingdom when Christ returns in the future, His kingdom, His reign, is also a *present reality*. This reality is at work within us, molding us into His image, filling us with love and joy and hope—even in the midst of tribulation. It is a love relationship with Christ, one which we enter at His invitation through repentance and faith. Those who belong to Christ are *in* His kingdom, are *entering* His kingdom, and *will inherit* His kingdom. It is present, it is ongoing, it is future, it is eternal.

Do you belong to Christ's kingdom?

At the Name of Jesus
*   Every knee shall bow,*
Every tongue confess Him
*   King of glory now;*
'Tis the Father's pleasure
*   We should call Him Lord,*
Who from the beginning
*   Was the mighty Word.*
                    —Caroline M. Noel

THE ADVANCEMENT OF GOD'S KINGDOM

You are the light of the world.
                    —Matthew 5:14

How does God's Kingdom advance, and whose responsibility is its advancement? Following the resurrection of Christ, before He ascended to heaven, He spoke these now well-known words to His disciples:

> All authority in heaven and on earth has been given to me. Go therefore and make disciples of all nations, baptizing them in the name of the Father and of the Son and of the Holy Spirit, teaching them to observe all that I have commanded you. And behold, I am with you always, to the end of the age.[90]

These words have come to be known as the Great Commission. There is probably no better summary in the Scriptures of what Jesus has instructed those who belong to Him to do. And there is no doubt that throughout the ages millions of devoted followers of Christ, inspired and enabled by this Great Commission, have engaged themselves in its faithful fulfillment. There is also no doubt that many Christians, including some who can quote this passage from memory and who believe that they already know almost everything that could be said about it, severely misunderstand and limit its meaning. They think that the Great Commission chiefly has to do with "missions"—whether to pray for missions, give to missions, or, in a rare case, go as a missionary.

The Great Commission is about the entire life and work of the Church, the day to day lives of God's people as they worship and serve Him. It is a Great Commission for Christian living. And while that does indeed include what may be called missions, it also includes family,

41

careers, time, money, character, loyalties, possessions, relationships, suffering, prayer, Bible study, identity, and spiritual gifts—all of life!

If your understanding of the Great Commission is only about "supporting missions," you do not understand the Great Commission. The Great Commission is to continue the work of Christ, filled and empowered and directed by the Spirit of Christ. The Great Commission gives direction to the entire life of a Christian, and it is certainly not anything that can be organized and steered, let alone be defined, by a church or denominational or para-church program or any humanly-organized program.

Let us briefly examine what Jesus said.

All authority in heaven and on earth has been given to me. This is the foundational statement of Christ for everything that followed in the Great Commission, and what an unspeakable tragedy it is that so many of those who claim to belong to Jesus have little conception of Christ's authority, little faith in it, little hope drawn from it, little joy found in it. Many Christians simply do not believe it, although they will say that they do. They would be much more excited and animated to know personally a well-known politician, or film star, or for that matter, anyone who is "in the news" than they are excited and animated to know and belong to Him who has all authority in heaven and on earth. They completely "buy into" the authority structures and appearances of the kingdom of the world while they assign no real significance to Jesus' own statement about Himself that all authority is His and no one else's. They look at the famous person's or successful person's or rich person's standing in the world as something that is "real" and as Jesus' authority as something that is "spiritual" or "religious." Is it then any wonder that their commitment to Him is so superficial and qualified?

Others live in a more devoted way unto Christ, but they do so as though they were following some tragic and defeated, if noble, figure. They have little belief in or understanding of His authority, that He is truly King of Kings and Lord of Lords, the Victor, the Conqueror of Sin and Death, not in some misty afterlife, but that Jesus is all those things right now. One day in a very definite future, all of the created order will kneel and every tongue confess that Jesus Christ is Lord, and Jesus has now the very same authority that He will have then. Jesus is neither tragic nor defeated, and those who serve Him should not act as if He were. It is those who reject Him in their pride and deceived condition who are tragic, and it is the devil who is defeated. But because many Christians lack a clear recognition of Jesus' true greatness and standing as Lord, they do not serve Him in the confidence and joy of faith of which Jesus is worthy and that He desires them to have.

Jesus has conquered the kingdom of this world, the rule of Satan, the works of the devil, that all who belong to Him may be rescued from the judgment that is coming upon the fallen world. The work of His people, His Church, is predicated upon His authority—and this does not mean the organized effort or authority of a congregation or denomination—that is second order. Every person who belongs to Him, every single believer belongs to this work with Christ as its Head, Jesus Christ who is the King of Kings. And this work, which we will examine further, goes forth in the name of Jesus Christ who has all authority in heaven and on earth. No one, no thing, no cause is higher or can even approach the status of the Lord Jesus Christ. And those who claim His name should both know it and rejoice in it.

Go therefore and make disciples of all nations. As great as Christian missions is in the service of Jesus Christ, and as powerful a mandate as this statement is to go forward in missionary work, this command of Christ to His disciples encompasses much more than missions. It is the life's work of all who belong to Christ.

A simple matter of translation often causes a misunderstanding of this passage. We should consider this statement more closely that its meaning may become clear.

First, in most English translations of this phrase the first verb is presented as an imperative, "go," when in fact, in the Greek, the verb is a participle: "going" or even more closely "having gone." This common translation as "go" clouds the sense of what Jesus was saying. Jesus was not, in this instance, specifically sending the disciples somewhere, He was telling them what to do *as they go forward* or *when they have departed.* He was telling them how to serve Him as they proceeded with their lives. Jesus was not referencing geography when He said "going" or "having gone". His emphasis was not to "go here" or "go there," but the sense of the phrase is something continuous "as you have gone forward" from here and with your lives.[91] And if a person understands this he gets the sense immediately, the correct sense, that this is an instruction for all disciples, not just for those who are missionaries.

The word "therefore" refers back to what Jesus said about His authority. So now we have Jesus telling us all, based upon His authority, based upon His being the Lord of all Creation, what we all are to do as we *go on* with our lives.

And what we are to do, all of us, is to *make disciples of all nations*. Let's look at the "all nations" part of this phrase first. The word translated "nations" might better be translated as "peoples". It is the word *ethne*, which has the same root as the English words ethnic and ethnicity. To immediately equate "nations" with "countries" is not the sense. Keep in mind that for the disciples in Jesus' day, there was only one "nation" of relevance in that sense: the Roman empire. When Paul went on his missionary journeys, it all took place within the Roman empire. The sense here is that the good news of salvation in Christ is for all people everywhere, whoever they are, wherever they are—people of all cultures and all walks of life.

Now the verb used for "make disciples" is indeed an imperative. But what does "make disciples" entail? Is not the entire New Testament written to "make disciples"? Are not all the gifts of the Holy Spirit given in order to help "make disciples"? Disciples are those who have given and are giving their whole lives with complete devotion to following, learning from, obeying, and modeling the character of someone else. Making disciples is a process. It takes time. It requires commitment. It needs correcting and improving and refining and maturing. As a person matures he comes to be, more and more, a true disciple. It is important to understand that to "make disciples" is an entirely different thing than merely to "make converts." Conversion, the initial step in following Christ, the first day of a new birth in Christ, can happen in a moment. Discipleship does not. The command to "make disciples" applies to those who do not know Christ at all, and it also applies *to those who do*! The Church, the people of God, are most certainly to take the message of Christ to those who have never heard so that they may believe and be saved. But that is only when the process of discipleship begins. Jesus' command to us to "make disciples" means that our life work in service to Him is to "encourage one another and build one another up"[92] in lives that are lived for Christ. We are to do this work in our homes, in our marriages, in our families, in our churches, in other relationships, in towns, cities, nations, and around the world. Because of who Christ is, the Lord of All and our Savior, as we go forward in our living, our command from Jesus is to proclaim that He is the King, He is Lord and Victor. We are to teach everyone everywhere to love, serve, and follow Him. This is not a religious component to our lives. This is the theme of our lives no matter who we are or what we do for a living.

That is the Great Commission. How we fulfill this Great Commission is the subject of a large part of the New Testament, and so I have no illusions about being able to cover it in this small book. But what I hope to do in the remaining chapters is to help you, if you need any help, in discovering how believing in and living for the kingdom of God through Christ will give guidance to your everyday life and bring His joy and purpose into all that you do.

Lift high the cross, the love of Christ proclaim
till all the world adore his sacred name.
—George W. Kitchin

THE ADVANCEMENT OF GOD'S KINGDOM THROUGH OUR MESSAGE

This is the message we have heard from him…
—1 John 1:5

We are all to do the work of making disciples. How do we do that, and what will that advancement look like?

A good place to begin as we seek to answer this question is to see how Jesus Himself sought to advance God's kingdom, and what that advancement looked like when He led it. What is rather astonishing is how often we Christians do not take this approach.

Jesus advanced God's kingdom through His message and through His life. We are to do the same. While we are not all called to preach, we are all called to have a message about Jesus Christ and live a life that demonstrates the truth of that message. Our message should agree with the message preached by Jesus Himself. And our lives are to be His very life in us.

So we will advance Christ's kingdom through what we have to say and through how we live. Let us first give attention to the message.

Jesus' preaching called people to repentance of sin and through that repentance, to new life, a life of love, faith, and obedience to God, all of which is made possible by Him personally and only by Him. Jesus' message was not changed by the Apostles as they began to preach. It has not changed to this very date. And the Gospel of Jesus Christ will never change.

But man's versions of that Gospel certainly do change. Just as there were corrupt versions of the Gospel being preached in the early church, there continue to be corrupt and even reprehensible versions of this message being preached today. And because these false versions of the gospel play well to men's conceit and pleasure, they generally get a good hearing.

Let us give some consideration to Jesus' message and what should, therefore, be our message about *repentance of sin*. Repentance means to turn away from, to leave, to abandon. Sin refers to anything we do and are that is against the will of God. And *sin* is inseparable from the salvation message of the entire Bible, from the first chapters of Genesis to the last chapter of Revelation. Sin is the explanation for man's brokenness, conflict, guilt, and condemnation—and Jesus Christ is God's answer to it. Jesus' death on the cross for our sins is an eternal sign both of God's judgment upon sin and His love, and Jesus' resurrection is an undying proof of hope, promise, and Jesus' victory over sin. Jesus preached that we must repent from sin, and He came to deliver us from its power.

There is no other doorway into the kingdom of God than the doorway of repentance of sin. A person who does not repent of his sins is not saved. This is not an obscure, dubious doctrine, questionably found in Scripture. It is at the core of the salvation message of the entire Bible and the preaching of Jesus Christ Himself. God accepts those who are truly sorry for their sin, who turn away from sin, and who seek His mercy and forgiveness. Jesus Christ, the sinless Son of God, came to *die*, and He died because of our sin. God's wrath will be revealed against men because of their sin. The problem with the world is its sin. God has judged sin. In His great love He has made provision to save us from the consequences of our condition before Him, but for those who reject that provision—for those who do not truly recognize their sin and hate it and cry out for God's mercy and forgiveness and turn away from lives of sin—there remains God's wrathful judgment. God will destroy with fire every trace of sin that every existed, He will create a new heaven and a new earth in which there is no sin, and those who are not found in the Lamb's book of life will be punished eternally away from His presence for their obstinate rejection of God's mercy. This is not an "old-fashioned" teaching, this is not a back-woods, redneck, hellfire and damnation message, this is the message of the Bible, of the Apostles, and of Christ Himself. No one should claim to preach or teach the gospel of Jesus Christ who does not preach and teach the truth about sin and the need for us to repent. It is actually difficult to imagine how someone who claims to be bearing the message of Jesus Christ could ignore and deny such foundational elements of that message as repentance, sin, and judgment.

But many do. It is tragic that many American preachers and teachers and authors today who claim to be proclaiming the gospel are attempting to do so without mentioning sin or repentance or salvation. In fact, it is some of the most famous, "successful," and popular preachers and Christian authors who never mention sin, or repentance, or judgment. Their messages range from encouragement about overcoming obstacles through faith—with an emphasis on how God is going to bless you and your life and your goals—to inoffensive (and that's important) suggestions to self-satisfied listeners on how one can make minor improvements to their already very fine spiritual walks. Their messages may contain social commentary, completely non-Biblical amalgams of pseudo-spiritual advice, or pop-psychological analysis. But no sin. No repentance. No judgment. No salvation.

The apostle Paul when writing the church at Corinth, who considered themselves to be very advanced in the faith, determined to preach only "Jesus Christ and Him crucified." An interested person can visit many churches today, watch many worship services on television, and read many Christian books and hear little to nothing about Jesus being crucified with all that the cross of Christ teaches us and represents. Sometimes they do not really hear that much about Jesus. But they will almost certainly hear flattery, receive motivational talks—sometimes quite effective ones, and receive some tips for successful American living.

Jesus did not come as a part of some grand divine self-help scheme to help Americans have more things, more worldly recognition, and more luxury. He did not come so one could be "O so blessed" with this and that and have everything he wants and meet all his goals and be a great success story. He came, first and foremost, to save our evil, selfish, greedy, lying, lustful, lazy, prideful, cowardly, despicable, sinful selves from eternal punishment and separation from God, which is what sinners deserve. And if you think that these words are strong, the Bible uses images for us and our sin that are stronger. Far stronger.

It is a wonderful truth that Jesus also came to give abundant life: to fill us with love and peace and kindness and goodness and patience and gentleness and humility and all the fruit of the Holy Spirit, which is the very character of Christ. He came in love that we cannot comprehend to give life forever in the presence of God and in a manner and a place that God has always intended. But the pathway, the only pathway, to experiencing the fullness of Christ, to receiving the gift of salvation and His very life within, is through true repentance from sin. John the Baptist was calling people to repentance, "but when he saw many of the Pharisees and Sadducees coming to his baptism, he said to them, 'You brood of vipers! Who warned you to flee from the wrath to come? Bear fruit in keeping with repentance.'"[93] Lip service or curiosity or casual affiliation is not enough. Coming to church is not enough. Baptism and communion are not enough. A person must recognize what it means to be a sinner, recognize that he is one, repent of His sin, and ask God for mercy and forgiveness. And a person who truly repents, when He receives the life of Christ and grows in discipleship, will experience as his life goes forward an ever-deepening realization of his sinfulness, his shameful condition before God, His dependency upon Christ for all that is good and holy, even though, in fact *because*, he is fully forgiven.

Repent does not mean "feel bad about." It does not mean to be sorry or be filled with regret. Sorrow and regret may lead to repenting. But sorrow and regret are not enough. To repent means to *quit!* To turn away from sin means that one no longer follows a path of sinful living. The Apostle John put this in very plain language:

> Little children, let no one deceive you. Whoever practices righteousness is righteous, as he is righteous. Whoever makes a practice of sinning is of the devil, for the devil has been sinning from the beginning. The reason the Son of God appeared was to destroy the works of the devil. No one born of God makes a practice of sinning, for God's seed abides in him, and he cannot

keep on sinning because he has been born of God. By this it is evident who are the children of God, and who are the children of the devil: whoever does not practice righteousness is not of God, nor is the one who does not love his brother.[94]

Jesus said that when the Holy Spirit comes, He will convict the world of sin, righteousness, and judgment[95] and that the Holy Spirit would glorify Jesus.[96] If our message is informed and led by the Holy Spirit, it will be one that recognizes the reality of sin and the requirement to repent if one is to know God. Many will reject God's call and resist the conviction that the Holy Spirit brings. But others will surrender to the conviction the Holy Spirit brings into their hearts, repent of their sins, and receive forgiveness and new life through faith in Christ. So as the kingdom of God advances, it does so in light of our message, and that message must include a call for all people everywhere to repent of their sin.

When you think of a person who has repented, erase from your mind images of a person who hates himself, who is always miserable, who sleeps on a bed of nails, who is judgmental of others, and who never smiles. On the contrary, a person who has repented, who truly has a repentant heart, will be a person who kind and loving, who has compassion for others, who is patient with other people and makes allowances for their faults, who often smiles and causes other people to smile as well, and who contributes to the lives of others in whatever ways that he is able. This is a person who rejects and turns away from selfishness, from seeing himself as his own God, from resentment, from hurting others, from trying to better himself at their expense, from ignoring and dishonoring the God who created us all, from hating, from envying, from greed, from gossip, and from sexual immorality. This is a person who decides to abandon all those behaviors and attitudes like grimy, sweaty, soiled clothes that have been worn for months on end. This is a person who asks to be washed and made clean by Christ and given new clothes as a gift—and who has no desire ever again to put on their former rags of filth. This will be a person who lives, increasingly so, as Christ lived and taught others to live. He is able to do so because Christ enables him through His presence within.

Was the message of Christ a call to faith in Himself? Indeed, it was—and it still is! But without a repentant heart, there is no faith. Faith in Christ for salvation can only occur when a person recognizes his need to be saved. He must admit his lost and sinful condition, confess his sin, repent of it, and look to Christ to do for him what he can never do for himself and for what he could never deserve.

Jesus preached repentance and faith. That is one way that He Himself advanced God's kingdom when He walked the earth. And it is still His message. If we are to advance God's kingdom as He has shown us, we, too, must bear the message to a sinful world, to sinful people, that they must repent and believe.

Jesus also advanced God's kingdom through how He lived. We must follow that example as well, and that is the subject of the next chapter.

Come, ye sinners, poor and wretched,
* Weak and wounded, sick and sore;*
Jesus ready stands to save you,
* Full of pity join'd with power;*
He is able, he is able, he is able;
* He is willing; doubt no more.*
                                    —*Joseph Hart*

The Advancement of God's Kingdom Through Our Living

By this we may know that we are in him: whoever says he abides in him ought to walk in the same way in which he walked.
—1 John 2:5-6

Repentance leads to new life—a life given us by Christ. And it is through our living this new life that the kingdom of God is advanced in the world. It is an advancement of people who are humble and contrite before God, not an advancement of pride, worldly recognition, and material success.

A person who repents has recognized the evil that is in the world and in himself and turns away from it to follow Christ to be given a different kind of life. This change comes about *following* repentance. Paul also writes to the Galatians, as a reminder, what their lives were like before coming to Christ and receiving His life and Spirit. He said

> Now the works of the flesh are evident: sexual immorality, impurity, sensuality, idolatry, sorcery, enmity, strife, jealousy, fits of anger, rivalries, dissensions, divisions, envy, drunkenness, orgies, and things like these. I warn you, as I warned you before, that those who do such things will not inherit the kingdom of God.[97]

Here is the same passage from the Phillips translation:

> The activities of the lower nature are obvious. Here is a list: sexual immorality, impurity of mind, sensuality, worship of false gods, witchcraft, hatred, quarrelling, jealousy, bad temper, rivalry, factions, party-spirit, envy, drunkenness, orgies and things like that. I solemnly assure you, as I

54

did before, that those who indulge in such things will never inherit God's kingdom.[98]

It is the life of Christ in us that replaces the old one for the person who has repented. The qualities of the life of Christ, produced in us by the Holy Spirit, are called the fruit of the Spirit. That fruit, we recall, is described by Paul in his letter to the Galatians:

> But the fruit of the Spirit is love, joy, peace, patience, kindness, goodness, faithfulness, gentleness, self-control; against such things there is no law.[99]

The kingdom of God advances as more and more people begin to live lives that can be characterized in this way. You contribute to God's kingdom by living a Spirit-filled, Spirit-led life. By living in humble obedience to God. By being a living example of God's love.

What does this advance look like? Well, it looks like farmers and ranchers and business people and teachers and civil servants and truckers and grocers and manufacturers and laborers and executives and scientists and musicians and physicians and attorneys and sailors and ministers, just for starters. It looks like all sorts of people from all sorts of cultures with all sorts of personalities and gifts and interests and pursuits. But there is a common thread in all of these people as God's Kingdom is advanced and that common thread is the very goodness of God Himself, given to us in Christ.

The kingdom of God, as it advances, doesn't look particularly "religious"—as many persons define and understand "religious." It looks much more like good people than it does religious people. It looks much more like beauty (real beauty) and kindness in living than it does religion in living. And it looks this way not because God has been left out, but because He is in it—and He is the Creator of beauty and the Source of goodness and kindness. It looks like people who love God and who love others and does not look like people who love their place of importance in the world, including in their religious organizations. Recall the interchange of a scribe (a religious expert) with Jesus:

> And one of the scribes … asked him, "Which commandment is the most important of all?" Jesus answered, "The most important is, 'Hear, O Israel: The Lord our God, the Lord is one. And you shall love the Lord your God with all your heart and with all your soul and with all your mind and with

all your strength.' The second is this: 'You shall love your neighbor as yourself.' There is no other commandment greater than these." And the scribe said to him, "You are right, Teacher. You have truly said that he is one, and there is no other besides him. And to love him with all the heart and with all the understanding and with all the strength, and to love one's neighbor as oneself, is much more than all whole burnt offerings and sacrifices." And when Jesus saw that he answered wisely, he said to him, "You are not far from the kingdom of God."[100]

This scribe's understanding had been enlarged to understand, truly, what the kingdom of God looked like: love for God and for one's neighbor more than "all burnt offerings and sacrifices" (religious practices). The scribe was referencing a Scripture from Hosea that he now more fully understood, "For I desire steadfast love and not sacrifice, the knowledge of God rather than burnt offerings."[101] On another occasion, Jesus referred some self-righteous, religious people to this same passage: "Go and learn what this means, 'I desire mercy, and not sacrifice.'"[102] On yet another occasion, Jesus and His disciples were criticized by some religious leaders because they broke some religious rules, rules that were man-made, but which were based on Scripture and which these leaders defended as the very will of God. Jesus said to them: "If you had known what this means, 'I desire mercy, and not sacrifice,' you would not have condemned the guiltless. For the Son of Man is lord of the Sabbath."[103] And these words from Jesus speak precisely as to how the kingdom of God looks as it advances and why. It does not look like more and more *religion*, as we often understand religion. It looks like more and more God-likeness—more goodness, kindness, justice, mercy, forgiveness, generosity, patience, joy, and more love in character and in living. It looks more and more like the life of Christ.

So is religion a good thing? Yes, indeed. But we have to be clear on what true religion really is and how "organized religion" (so-called) relates to true religion. Since we can only touch on such a large topic here, let us at least establish a fact or two.

Jesus said of Himself that the "Son of Man is Lord of the Sabbath"— the Sabbath representing religious practices. This points to the truth that any religious practice, for any people, for any time, culture, history, or rationale is validated by whether or not it brings glory to Christ and truly nurtures, or builds up, the life of Christ within His people.

Bear in mind, that just as the religious leaders in Jesus' day defended their view of keeping the Sabbath laws—in the name of God and Scripture and all that is holy—people will defend today even the most provincial, legalistic, offensive, silly, far-fetched, ignorant, and exclusionary religious views with the same zeal and stubbornness. They will say that, by definition, comporting with their religious practices and doctrines (especially their doctrines) glorifies Christ and builds up His people, no matter how un-Christlike their behavior or how sectarian their doctrine. Unlike what Scripture teaches, they seem to believe that God values "sacrifice" (religious practice) over "mercy."

True followers of Christ do indeed engage in particularly religious practices, some instituted by Christ Himself, that are beautiful, essential, joy-filled, and are as varied as are God's people. Prayers, praises, preaching and teaching of God's word, the Lord's table, nurture of children, and mutual encouragement are just a few examples. These practices bring glory to Christ and build up His people because those who are engaging in them belong to Christ and are doing so to worship Him, to serve Him, to love Him, and to love and serve others. But no religious practice is legitimate if it fails to glorify Christ, goes against His will, discredits or misrepresents His character, or seeks to substitute "sacrifice" for "mercy."

People are won to Christ through the Christlike living of those who know Him. The world is changed for the better through the very presence of Christ, who still walks the earth through the lives of His people. It is not a matter of churches getting bigger, it is a matter of people becoming Christlike. The advancement of God's kingdom is not a matter of people joining something, it is a matter of them receiving something—and that something is Christ Himself and the life that He offers.

Jesus said "The wind blows where it wishes, and you hear its sound, but you do not know where it comes from or where it goes. So it is with everyone who is born of the Spirit."[104] That this is how the kingdom of God advances. Does that divine process sound like institutional development attained through advertising, vision statements, mission statements, enrollments, market studies, meetings, and goal setting? In fact, does it sound like anything that man is doing, including what is sometimes called religion? The growth of God's kingdom is the Spirit's work. He is not looking to us to organize it but to participate in it in faithful, humble, obedient love.

True religion is of the heart and is expressed in the way a person lives, empowered by the Spirit of God. And so we can see that "religion" cannot be organized at all, except insofar as a life itself can be organized. Some things that we do together as followers of Christ can be organized—of course. But religion itself is a condition of the person and his relationship with God through Christ.

Jesus attended the synagogue on the Sabbath. And although He broke some religious laws and traditions of men that were being misrepresented as laws of God, it is certainly accurate to say that Jesus participated in and gave conditional support to organized religion. But that is not how he changed the world. Jesus did not change the world because he faithfully attended synagogue and completed religious observances. He changed the world through the power of His life, including the power of His message. The Apostle Peter speaking of Jesus said "God anointed Jesus of Nazareth with the Holy Spirit and with power. He went about doing good and healing all who were oppressed by the devil, for God was with him."[105] Peter did not say anything about Jesus being regular in synagogue attendance or how He kept the feasts, although no doubt He was and did. But Jesus advanced God's kingdom through His life. And if you belong to Him, so will you. Just by being you, as God has created you and enabled you to be.

There actually is, however, an organization to all of this, and if you belong to Christ you are part of that organization. That is the subject of the next chapter.

Take my life, and let it be
Consecrated, Lord, to Thee.
Take my moments and my days;
Let them flow in ceaseless praise.
              —Frances R. Havergal

WHO DOES WHAT IN GOD'S KINGDOM?

Having gifts that differ according to the grace given to us, let us use them.

—Romans 12:6

If you desire to experience joy and fulfillment in your relationship with God and know that you are where you are meant to be in the advancement of His kingdom, there is good news for you. The Bible gives clear teachings on the organization of God's work and knowing your place in it.

The organization of God's kingdom is a spiritual organization. It is real—more real than any human organization could be—and it is *spiritual*. God is Spirit.[106] He has sent the Holy Spirit to give life to His people. And the organization of His people is a spiritual one, administered by the Holy Spirit Himself, with Christ as its Head. This organization is not and does not resemble a corporation, or a bureaucracy, or a school, or a business, or an entertainment production, or a political party, or a government, or even a typical religious hierarchy. The organization of the kingdom of God is compared in Scripture to a human body, with Christ as its head, and with each one of us as being various parts, i.e. members, of that human body. And nowhere does God tell us that His organization of the Church, a spiritual body, can or may be subordinated to the hundreds and thousands of organizational structures that men manage to come up with. God's Church is not organized "within the context" of our organizations. Our "organizational charts" mean nothing to Heaven. The Church is eternal, the Body of Christ, the Bride of Christ, enlivened and indwelled by the Spirit of

60

Christ, with each member contributing to the living Church in ways that are assigned by the Holy Spirit.

All this is written in the Bible for your instruction, encouragement, and benefit. It is written to inform you and direct you to know what to expect in God's organization, to know that you are a member of this body, and to know what "part" of the body you are, so that you can understand how God has designed and gifted you to serve Him. And you will not find complete joy or fulfillment in your life as a Christian until and unless you understand where you fit in to this body, the body of Christ.

Someone may object to such a sweeping statement and argue that many Christians throughout the ages have found joy and fulfillment in knowing Christ and that they have done so without conceptualizing their lives as a functioning part of a spiritual body. And I am in complete agreement. But let us also agree that a person may not have the least idea of what air or oxygen is, may have no idea how the lungs work or how blood is kept healthy, and that person nevertheless enjoys great benefits from breathing. In a similar way, if a person is living a fulfilled life in Christ and is serving Him effectively, that person is functioning in His body according to His divinely-assigned role in it, whether He knows it or not.

In explaining what the Church is and how it operates, Paul wrote to the Christians in Corinth:

> To each is given the manifestation of the Spirit for the common good. For to one is given through the Spirit the utterance of wisdom, and to another the utterance of knowledge according to the same Spirit, to another faith by the same Spirit, to another gifts of healing by the one Spirit, to another the working of miracles, to another prophecy, to another the ability to distinguish between spirits, to another various kinds of tongues, to another the interpretation of tongues. All these are empowered by one and the same Spirit, who apportions to each one individually as he wills.

> For just as the body is one and has many members, and all the members of the body, though many, are one body, so it is with Christ.[107]

This letter was written to *all* Christians in Corinth—not just to some. And when Paul says "To *each* is given the manifestation of the Spirit for the common good," he means exactly that. Each Christian has been given a manifestation—a gift[108]—of the Spirit that is to be used for the good of the entire body of Christ. Later in the same letter, to reinforce the teaching, he writes "Now you are the body of Christ and individually members of it."[109]

Your service to God is not so much a matter of having tasks assigned to you as it is realizing who you actually are. A hand does not "do the work of" a hand; it *is* a hand. And so it grips, helps, waves, pats the backs of others—does all the things that a hand does because it is a hand. An eye does not choose to see or respond to someone's request for it to see. It sees because it is an eye. Now a hand may be tasked to do a certain thing that hands do. An eye may be tasked to look at a particular thing, since it is an eye that has the ability to look. But these members of the body are still functioning, in obedience, according to *what they are*. And your service to God, if indeed you function according to your true place in His kingdom, will be in accordance with *who you are*, who He has created you and gifted you to be.

The manifestation of the Holy Spirit in your life—the gift of the Spirit—becomes a part of your very person, and when you exercise that gift, when you allow the Holy Spirit to manifest His work and presence through you, you will feel to a large degree that you are "being yourself." You are not just doing what you are gifted to do, you are being *who* you are gifted to *be*. You will find joy in your living and in your service, first of all because it will fit the very nature that God has given you, and secondly because you will be very effective in building up God's people as you are doing and being what God has ordained and is blessing.

Before we go any further, try and comprehend what an important, what an indispensible and vital teaching this is, if Paul's inspired teaching is true...and it most certainly is true. Paul is describing what it actually means for a person to belong to Christ and to be a part of His Church—His body. This is the very key to joy and fulfillment in service to Jesus Christ—to live in accordance with one's gift, to live in surrender, in cooperation, and in understanding of the manifestation of the Spirit that one has been given. If this is true, how is a person supposed to function in God's Church or contribute or prioritize his time if he is trying to do so without the simple and essential benefit of knowing what his gift is? If he has not recognized the manifestation of the Spirit in His life? How can he do so if he does not know whether he is a hand or a foot or an eye? Conversely, we can easily recognize the simple beauty and efficiency of each person knowing what he is gifted to do and pursuing the use of his gift in joyful service, although that pursuit will certainly have its challenges. If the body of Christ may be compared to an orchestra, it is obvious that each member must know (at least) what instrument he plays. And we can also see how unimaginable it would be for a person to say he is a member of the orchestra but have no idea what instrument he plays or, for that matter, not even know whether he is able to play one at all.

So this teaching is basic. Fundamental. Foundational. It should be the common understanding of each member of the body of Christ, and yet it is a teaching that is scandalously marginalized, ignored or even corrupted throughout the Church today. A Christian can attend some[110] churches from cradle to grave and never be taught to recognize his spiritual gift and to use his spiritual gift throughout his life in the service of Christ. The subject may not come up at all, let alone be taught as foundational. And yet that same Christian may be bombarded with myriads upon myriads of general appeals to join this or join that, to attend, to attend, to attend, to be on a committee or a board, to show up for an activity, to be a part of a class, to help with projects, and on and on and on. And in the midst of these institutional requests and demands, some Christians will manage to find a match, or something resembling a match, for their true gifts to what the institution needs or promotes or organizes. But others—many others—live week to week and year to year frustrated because they have a heart to serve God and a love for Him, but there just doesn't appear to be an opportunity for them to serve God in a way that seems to fit who they are. They feel guilty because they never think that they are "doing enough" for the institution to which they belong...or for God. And they do not see, indeed they have never been taught to understand, how they may be called to serve God with their own particular gifts in ways that may or may not come under a particular heading or category or ministry or committee or board or program of the organization to which they belong.

Volunteerism in the Church, as well-intended as it may be, and as necessary as it may be for getting certain tasks done, is a poor and haphazard substitute for understanding and facilitating the use of spiritual gifts. Let's look at some problems with it.

First, volunteerism is extremely limiting—even with so-called mega-churches that may offer dozens and dozens of opportunities for which one can volunteer. The opportunities are still, by definition, activities that the institution is organizing—and the entire work of the body of Christ in this world cannot be encompassed within such a structure. If someone has the gift of exhortation, i.e. encouragement, he needs help in knowing how to put that gift into practice, woven into his daily lifestyle and circumstances. Most churches don't have an Encouragement Committee (although there are occasionally some groups that function as Discouragement Committees). The gift of encouragement might in some ways be systematically exercised, but it cannot be packaged and run exclusively though church programs and subgroups. Volunteerism often results in the wrong people volunteering—they do so because they are willing to help or they have the time or they are seeking affirmation or what have you. Perhaps they just hate to "stand by" and see an alleged institutional need go unmet. And so they volunteer to devote time and energy to a project for which they are not particularly qualified, causing them, necessarily, to neglect exercising their true gifts in ways that would be much more beneficial to the body of Christ. Volunteerism usually results in overloading the willing with busyness. A small percentage of a group's membership normally volunteers to do most of the work. Volunteerism is never satisfied, because there is no end to the number of ideas people can develop if only there will be enough volunteers! And finally, a culture, a mindset, of volunteerism, appropriate in many contexts, is inappropriate to the service of Christ. Christians are servants, not volunteers. We are bought with a price,[111] we are not self-owned, autonomous persons who are graciously tipping God with some of our time and energy. Our gifts from the Holy Spirit are blessings of love and grace, manifestations of His very work and presence in our lives. It is offensive and absurd for us to think of these undeserved gifts and our use of them in the same way we think of being asked if we feel like "volunteering" for this or that. Do you think that servants should be asked to "volunteer" to serve? God doesn't either.

What God has done for us in Christ through the gifts of the Holy Spirit is to give us ways to serve His kingdom that are chosen by Him especially for us. What could be better than to know that one is using a gift that was selected and given personally to him by the Holy Spirit Himself? And God's giftedness to His people encompasses all that He desires the Church to do and to be—not just at the meeting-houses, and not just in ways that are organized at the meeting houses.

We will look at spiritual gifts in more detail in the next chapter.

Veni, creator Spiritus
mentes tuorum visita,
imple superna gratia,
quae tu creasti pectora.
—Rabanus Maurus, attr.

(Come, Holy Ghost, Creator blest,
and in our hearts take up Your rest;
Come with Your grace and heav'nly aid,
to fill the hearts which You have made.)

FULFILLING YOUR ROLE IN GOD'S KINGDOM

Fan into flame the gift of God, which is in you.
—2 Timothy 1:6

The Church is indeed organized. But many Christians are confused or misinformed about how it is organized and, therefore, they are frustrated by an unfulfilled Christian walk. This confusion can be cleared up. God does not desire us to be ignorant[112] of His plan for our lives. He desires us to understand our citizenship in His kingdom and the work that He has gifted each of us to do.

The Church is a spiritual body, the body of Christ, not an enterprise, and the mission of the Church is to live in the name and the power of Christ, making disciples of all peoples. The organizer of the Church is the Holy Spirit with Christ as the Head. And the work of the Church takes place wherever God's people are living in surrendered obedience to Christ. Each member of the church is to exercise his gift to contribute to the work of the whole, and it is the Holy Spirit who assigns the gifts. He does so in such a way, in such a deep way, that our giftedness becomes integral to who we are. If the Holy Spirit desires you to paint, He does not just place a paint brush in your hands, He makes you to be a painter—someone who is able to paint, who wants to paint, and who is successful at painting. A person undoubtedly will grow and improve in learning to use his gift. He may need formal training (or he may not). But in all cases the gift is a calling that becomes a part of the person. It is not an awkward, ill-fitting task or assignment. It is you being you in Christ. And Christ living His life through you.

What are these gifts and how do you know what your gift is? Let's take the first question first.

There are principally three areas in the New Testament where spiritual gifts are discussed in some detail. They are Romans 12, 1 Corinthians 12-14, and Ephesians 4. In all three passages, you will find a consistent teaching that each believer has a spiritual gift and that he should utilize that gift wholeheartedly for the building up of the church. You will also find the consistent teaching that God's love is more important than any spiritual gift and that His love must be the context for the use of our gifts.

In each of these passages a list of spiritual gifts appears. It is not the same list, but there are commonalities among the three. None of these lists is meant to be complete and exhaustive, but in each case Paul is giving examples of spiritual gifts. For this reason, as you seek to understand your spiritual gift, it is not imperative that you find your spiritual gift represented exactly on one of these Biblical lists although they are undoubtedly the place to start. Let's look at the relevant passage from Romans:

> For as in one body we have many members, and the members do not all have the same function, so we, though many, are one body in Christ, and individually members one of another. Having gifts that differ according to the grace given to us, let us use them: if prophecy, in proportion to our faith; if service, in our serving; the one who teaches, in his teaching; the one who exhorts, in his exhortation; the one who contributes, in generosity; the one who leads, with zeal; the one who does acts of mercy, with cheerfulness.[113]

As you can see, Paul does not even mention here some gifts we might expect to see since they figure prominently in Corinthians and Ephesians, such as apostles and miracles. And he mentions some examples of gifts here that do not appear elsewhere, such as exhortation (encouragement), giving, leading, and showing acts of mercy.

A key to understanding the manifold diversity of spiritual gifts is the introduction that Paul gives in the Corinthian letter:

> Now there are varieties of gifts, but the same Spirit; and there are varieties of service, but the same Lord; and there are varieties of activities, but it is the same God who empowers them all in everyone.[114]

This passage contains plain and literal truth to be sure, but the language and structure go far beyond the literal. The language is poetical as well and is rich in implication. First of all, it is Trinitarian: the "same Spirit," the "same Lord," the "same God". We already gain the sense that as Paul is explaining spiritual gifts, He is describing the very presence of the Godhead working in and through the Church, the body and Bride of Christ. Added to this, he uses a triad of descriptors to explain how God manifests Himself in His people: varieties of *gifts*, varieties of *service*, and varieties of *activities*. God's gifts of Himself to His people are representative of His limitless beauty, power, energy, diversity, and loving purposes. And so it bears repeating that as you seek to understand what your spiritual gift is, the lists of examples that appear in Scripture are there for your instruction and you may find your spiritual gift right there. Or, your spiritual gift may be something that is fully consistent with Scripture and with God's character and purposes, but which does not seem to be exactly defined by any one of the examples that we find in the three lists.

Before I suggest how to discover what your spiritual gift is, we need to dispense with some common misperceptions.

A spiritual gift is an ability we receive from God to use to contribute to the life and work of the Church. It is not a talent—although God may decide to use one's talents as a part of his gift. For example, a person may be a talented speaker, but his spiritual gift may or may not be preaching and teaching. If it is, then his talent for speaking may be used to strengthen his gift—although quite often, God will choose to use a person who has little *natural* talent for speaking to become an effective teacher. The Apostle Paul himself was, apparently, not a "dynamic speaker,"[115] and the Lord used him.

A spiritual gift is not a natural personality type or characteristic. An assertive person does not necessarily have the gift of leadership; actually his assertiveness probably makes it less likely. For that matter, it does not follow at all that a person who is a recognized leader in business or government has the *spiritual* gift of leadership. Let's explore this a bit further, since some will desire to take issue. They would say, for example, that "leadership" outside the church translates into "leadership" within the church. Leadership is leadership. Aren't spiritual gifts a part of our personhood, such that they feel natural to us, like a hand being a hand? Or a leader being a leader?

Yes, they are. But they are a part of our *new* personhood in Christ, our reborn personhood. And they are *gifts to* that personhood from God Himself, not innate talents or inclinations. Spiritual gifts are given for the good of the Church, and that includes for the good of the recipient. It is often the case, that a person who may have great leadership responsibilities and demonstrated abilities in the world is given a spiritual gift that places him in a helping or a facilitating role in the life of the Church. The Holy Spirit knows and has His reasons for the assignment of gifts, but one can see how, in this example, such assignments help the church, for these persons can be extremely effective helpers, givers, and facilitators. The gift also helps the person himself as it cultivates a spirit of love and servanthood that he finds to be a blessing to his life and very much a part of his true, redeemed personhood, his new self, in Christ. So, in short, a person's role in affairs of the world outside of the life of the church does not reveal his spiritual giftedness. It is not even a strong indicator.

Another common error regarding spiritual gifts occurs when people take some version of a personality or interest inventory, see what is indicated, and then make the leap to assume that this result points to their spiritual gifts as well. God doesn't work that way. God is redeeming us (saving us, buying us back) and he is sanctifying us (making us holy, shaping us into the image of Christ, putting to death our old self and giving life to our new self). Our spiritual gifts are a part of this process. God does not cater to our personality preferences and interests. To the degree that sin in all of its manifestations is a part of our personality preferences and interests, His will is that those inclinations be put to death. Eradicated. And so, our spiritual gifts may be in surprising contrast to what we "would have guessed." The apostle John along with his brother James were nicknamed by Jesus "Sons of Thunder"[116]—apparently because of their personalities, perhaps even their tempers! And yet John, in Christ, became the apostle who perhaps more eloquently than any other and with a fatherly tone wrote immortal words about the compassionate, tender love of God. The Apostle Paul, because of his background as a zealous Pharisee, would have seemed to be the obvious person to explain the gospel to the Jewish people. I think it seemed that way even to Paul himself. And yet it was Paul, the last person anyone would have chosen for this assignment, whom God chose to spearhead the effort to take the gospel to the Gentiles. One may make the point that Paul's leadership skills were manifest both before and after his conversion. To that I must respond that the difference between "leading" an armed entourage who terrorized and brutalized helpless Christians and their families and that of "leading" a missionary work while, for years, being beaten, stoned, pursued, imprisoned, hungry, exposed, ridiculed, abandoned, shipwrecked, and ill—the difference between these two models of "leadership" is so profound that surely no one can seriously view them as the same thing.

How do we know what gift we have?

Spiritual gifts are not determined or discerned by worldly pursuits, talents, natural interests or inclinations. They are determined by God who does not consult with anyone about His decisions and who has His own reasons for assigning spiritual gifts as He does. If you desire to know your spiritual gift, turn first to God Himself in that inquiry and forget about what makes sense to you based upon your resumé, personality, and religious interests.

Are there some practical steps? Certainly. The Bible's teaching on this subject are intended to be practical—applied to our living. That's the point really. But because the body of Christ is a spiritual body, because we are contending with spiritual realities, the "practical" steps have a great deal to do with our spiritual lives. This may present a problem for persons who consider that only material, "concrete" things are really "practical." Paul writes about and to those folks, as well. The entire second chapter of the first letter to the Corinthians is devoted to spiritual wisdom and he concludes those particular thoughts with the following:

> But I, brothers, could not address you as spiritual people, but as people of the flesh, as infants in Christ. I fed you with milk, not solid food, for you were not ready for it. And even now you are not yet ready, for you are still

of the flesh. For while there is jealousy and strife among you, are you not of the flesh and behaving only in a human way?[117]

And unfortunately this message is still appropriate to many a Christian or even congregation today.

So the first *practical* step toward understanding and using your spiritual gifts is to surrender your entire life to God in love and humility and with a repentant heart. You don't do this once; you do it daily. Constantly. And if you have not done this or are not doing this, don't expect a great deal of insight about knowing and using your spiritual gift, although what God reveals is certainly up to Him. God is not going to chat with you, man to man, about what you might be able to do for Him or how you can help His kingdom's work. He doesn't need your help. You need His help. And the fact that He would send His Holy Spirit into any of our lives is an act of incomprehensible love and grace. That the Holy Spirit of God would manifest Himself through our lives should keep us continuously humble and grateful. As we surrender ourselves to him, give up self will, and allow His will to be our own, He will reveal not only His gifts to us but the avenues for their use.

As we surrender our lives to Christ and seek to understand what gift has been given to us by the Holy Spirit, the following activities and considerations will be helpful: Prayer, God's Word, Opportunity, and Affirmation.

PRAYER

It is God's will for you to know what gift He has given you. Through prayer, including the outcomes of your prayer, God will surely show you. Seek God in prayer on this issue. Ask Him, in simple, trusting faith, to reveal your gift to you. He will do it.

> If any of you lacks wisdom, let him ask God, who gives generously to all without reproach, and it will be given him. But let him ask in faith, with no doubting, for the one who doubts is like a wave of the sea that is driven and tossed by the wind. For that person must not suppose that he will receive anything from the Lord; he is a double-minded man, unstable in all his ways.[118]

This answer may come over a period of time and seeking, or it may come rather quickly. It may come through a variety of means that the Lord will use. But as you surrender your life to God and seek this answer in prayer, He will reveal to you what your spiritual gift is.

GOD'S WORD

Studying God's word is actually a part of prayer regarding spiritual gifts and, for that matter, any other prayer issues. We need to study the passages in scripture that teach about spiritual gifts. And we need to study His word generally that we may be strengthened and mature in our spiritual life and discipleship. There is a process of help and revelation that occurs as we spend time with God in His word in which God addresses us holistically, not just on whatever point may be foremost in our minds. As you study God's word, are built up in the faith, and taught more and more about living in Christ, you begin to have a context of mind and heart into which God is able then to reveal to you what your spiritual gift is and how to use it.

You cannot expect to "look up" your spiritual gift in the Bible in the way you might look up the father of Abraham or the Song of Simeon! But it is certainly possible that as you read about the spiritual gifts that are listed in Scripture, the Lord will show you that your gift is one of those that are listed. This revelation will probably not come in a flash of insight or instruction, although it could. It is more likely that such a revelation will be a divine confirmation and naming of what you have already sensed and experienced as you walk in surrender and obedience to Christ.

Any spiritual gift, whether "listed" or not, will be in complete harmony with God's word and everything taught there about the church and about Christ. Remember that a spiritual gift comes from God Himself, and so it will always be in agreement with all that He has revealed. And a spiritual gift is something that is used to build up the Church—for the common good.

For example, if a person said that his spiritual gift is to comfort those who are rejecting Christ by telling them there will be no judgment—no consequences—then that person is sorely mistaken. Such a "gift" would be contrary both to God's word and to His expressed character. It fails the test of being in agreement with God's word and with the life and teachings of Christ.

But suppose a musician—an instrumental musician—believes that his spiritual gift is performing music in the worship of God, something that gives praise to God and uplifts the hearers. That is quite possible, even though "instrumental music" does not appear on a Biblical list of spiritual gifts. It is particularly plausible if that person has been utilizing his gift of music in just that way, and God is being praised, and God's people are being lifted up in their spirits. Of course there will be some who would try to make this gift fit under the "heading" of one of the listed gifts, no matter how much of a stretch that is. (When all else fails, it can always be listed under "helps"!) But music is not on the list. The use of music in this fashion is, however, Biblically-supported both by precept and example. It is consistent with God's character (who created music), and it is supported empirically since many Christians clearly are helped and strengthened by it. And even though musical skill is a talent, when God so decides, the use of a talent can certainly be brought into His service.

OPPORTUNITY

Some strong indicators regarding one's spiritual gift are the opportunities for serving God that are presented to us as we follow Christ in surrendered living. But as you assess those opportunities, some things should be clarified immediately.

When considering what your opportunities are for serving God, use caution regarding those things you have been "asked to do" at a church. Sometimes (not always, but sometimes) the things you are "asked to do" are monumental distractions, devised by that dangerous group, well-meaning others, that will significantly interfere with your ability actually to exercise your true spiritual gift. Also, some things you are "asked to do" may flatter you and fan the fires of your vanity because they represent your perceived standing or importance or influence in your community, as in the classic formula: Chairman of the Corporate Board=Chairman of the Deacons or Elders. But this invitation to transfer your worldly importance into the leadership of a congregation may not even resemble the spiritual gift that the Holy Spirit has actually given to you. It is a certainty that God does not flatter us or stroke our vanities. Not with spiritual gifts and not in any other way.

Instead, when you consider your opportunities for serving God, think of the thing that you can do, using the means that are at your disposal— both personal and material, using the ideas and insights that you have, to *build other Christians up in Christ and to demonstrate the love and message of Christ*. Forget what "position" you would like to hold in an institution—including a church. Forget where you can make your mark in the organization. What is the thing that you can do, and you know you can do even if it makes you nervous to think about, using the means that are at your disposal—both personal and material, using the ideas and insights that you have, to *build other Christians up in Christ and to demonstrate the love and message of Christ.*

For example, let's revisit the example of encouragement. You may be an encourager. You are able to spot people who are down and need a lift, and you enjoy saying a word to them to pick them up. Not only that, but people that you know come to your mind—you're not sure why or how—and you just feel a certainty that a note or a phone call to a certain person, to encourage him, would be a good idea. Sometimes you seem to know just what to write or say although you aren't sure how you know. And when you make a call or write a note, you have an inner joy and assurance that what you are doing is a good thing. Reflecting on your spiritual walk in this way is how to consider your "opportunities." Reflect upon your opportunities to help build up the people who comprise the church or to advance the work of Christ in the world. It may or may not have anything to do with an official position in a congregational organization.

Here is another example. You may have a love for visiting people who are shut in or ill or just lonely. Although some people begin to tremble and their knees knock together when they think about making a visit, you love to do it. You look forward to it. You know that it brings a blessing to the people you visit, and it brings a blessing to you as you fulfill this ministry. There may indeed be an organized congregational ministry of visitation that you can be a part of. And if you can do so, wonderful! But suppose the congregational program is, essentially, a Monday night event, and you can't go out on Monday nights because of a family or work obligation. In such a case, do *not* look for "something else" or another way to do ministry. Do not be controlled by institutional schedules. God's gifts in this area are not just for those who have Monday nights open! And they are not just for people who can be a part of an organized program. Or perhaps in your congregation, this would be an expectations of deacons, and you are not a deacon. Never mind about that. God has given you this gift. He chose it for you. He desires you to use it. He will go before you and bless you as you do so. Do not hesitate to use your gift faithfully. You will simply be exercising your gift at a time that does not line up with a congregational program or that is not restricted by congregational structures and the myriad of confused ideas and expectations that can be attached to them. God knows what He is doing. You might find someone to go with you who has the same gift—or a complementary gift, such as a person of discernment or one who is mighty in prayer. Form a small team. But use your gift. God wants you to. That is why you have it. And do so according to the opportunities that *God* has provided or leads you to develop.

AFFIRMATION

Another helpful indicator regarding our spiritual gift is that of affirmation from others. But this statement is dangerously unqualified and open to misinterpretation, so it must be further explained.

Affirmation does not mean praise or flattery or even approval. If we are receiving personal praise, it should raise a red flag. It may indicate that we are calling attention more to ourselves than to Christ, that we are seeking more to make a personal impression (and successfully so) than we are to build someone up in the Lord. Flattery is never a good thing. Flattery is used by the devil to manipulate us for his purposes. There is always a hook hidden within flattery, a hook into our pride that makes it hard later to disappoint the flatterer, because we don't want to lose that feeling we receive when we are flattered. And invariably we will be drawn into making a choice between compromising our principles or losing the flattery. Bear in mind that God never flatters us. Approval itself may or may not be an indicator that we are using out gift as God has intended. It completely depends on who is giving or withholding the approval. Remember that the Apostle Paul said regarding the use of his gift (apostleship) that if he were still trying to receive the approval of people he could not be a servant of God.[119] And he meant, primarily, the approval of *religious* people.

The kind of affirmation that matters is the kind that shows you that in using your gift you are helping to build up the body of Christ and do the work of Christ. It may indeed come from the mouths of others who, in sincerity, let you know that what you are doing or have done has lifted them up in the Lord, has blessed their lives, has helped strengthen their faith, has helped them better to know Christ and His love and helped them to live for Him. Other people who walk with the Lord and who know you will help you to know your gift by encouraging you in the effectiveness or in the potential that they see in you. Guidance from those who are wise and committed to Christ will play an important role in your understanding of your spiritual giftedness.

There may also be times when most of your affirmation comes from God Himself who affirms in your heart and mind that you are serving Him as He desires, that He is pleased with it, and that you can trust Him about it, even if others do not notice or affirm you in any way. Jesus taught that we should not practice our righteousness to be seen by men. The use of some gifts is more visible than others, even if no one is seeking public exposure. But it is almost a certainty that much of your life's devotion to God, including how you exercise your spiritual gift, will not be seen or recognized by others. And so, while there may be limited affirmation from people, God will give you His own affirmation. And "your Father who sees in secret will reward you."[120]

If you surrender your life to God, and if you seek the knowledge of your spiritual gift through prayer, studying God's word, opportunities God provides, and affirmation from trustworthy sources, it will be made clear to you what gift you have and, with that knowledge, you can go forward in a journey of using your gift in the role that God Himself has given you in His kingdom's work.

As you do so, however, it is time to revisit some issues that were raised at the beginning of this book. In particular, we need to review how we conceptualize what it means to "be a Christian" in this world that we live in. We will do so in the next chapter.

Living for Jesus who died in my place,
Bearing on Calv'ry my sin and disgrace;
Such love constrains me to answer His call,
Follow His leading, and give Him my all.
—Thomas O. Chisholm

THE TWO KINGDOMS: MAKING THE CHOICE

No one can serve two masters.
                    —Matthew 6:24

On June 6, 1944, the largest military invasion force ever assembled crossed the English Channel and, at great human sacrifice, successfully established a beachhead in Normandy. Through this beachhead began to pour the Allied Forces that liberated Western Europe from the Nazi-controlled, Axis Powers. The successful invasion at Normandy signaled the beginning of the end for the Nazis, but the war was still far from over. The Allied forces had to advance for hundreds of miles, sometimes against desperate resistance and fierce assault, until Nazi Germany was successfully subdued and final victory was achieved.

The men who comprised this invading force—all of them—knew several things with complete certainty. They knew there was a war going on, and they knew that they were in it. They knew which side they were on and that there was no place whatsoever for divided loyalties. They knew to expect hardship and sacrifice, even the ultimate sacrifice, and that the cause for which they were engaged required it.

We Christians are also in a war. We are in a war to liberate people everywhere from the bondage of the devil. In the name of Christ, we are to advance on Satan's empire and set its captives free. As citizens of the kingdom of God, it is our mission, all of us, to invade the kingdom of this world. Our Lord Jesus Christ has already established the "beachhead" by His life, death, and resurrection. We are to follow Him in His work to destroy the works of the devil and make disciples of all peoples. Even more assuredly than the Nazis' fate having been sealed by the invasion of Normandy, the fate of the devil's kingdom was sealed by the cross of Christ. Yes, the Church still has work to do, some miles yet to go, as God brings all those into His Church who are among the elect and brings the earth's history to an end. But even as this war is brought to its conclusion, the outcome has already been determined. The devil's time is short, and he knows it. Jesus Christ is the Victor!

But what kind of an army are we! Those who fought World War II knew that a war was on and that they were in it. Do we? Or have we become so comfortable in the camp that we have forgotten to engage the enemy? Or even forgotten that there is an enemy? Regarding His Church, Jesus said that the gates of hell will not prevail against it. That is a picture of a Church that is storming the gates of a kingdom whose resistance will not prevail. But are we storming the gates? Do we even see ourselves in that way? "Make disciples of all nations." That is our mission—each one of us and all of us together. And the very act of making disciples means that the devil's strongholds must be overcome. But they will not be overcome by an army that does not even acknowledge that a war is on. Nor will hell be overcome when the individuals who do acknowledge the war refuse, nevertheless, to recognize that they themselves are in it.

It is hardly possible even to think of a person in the Allied invasion force in 1944 who did not know which side he was on or who divided his loyalties and activities between the two sides. It is a ridiculous idea that soldiers who fought on a Monday for the Allies might have put in a day for the Nazis on Tuesday and then returned to the Allied forces on Wednesday. Allied forces were not confused in their mission nor did they identify with the enemy and his cause.

But what about the Church today? Does the American Church truly appear to be "called out" of the world? Do we know whose side we are on and is it obvious to all that we do? Or does the American Church often seem to be very much a part of this world, much like other institutions and enterprises—just a "religious" one? Do its members live as those who know a conflict is going on all around them?

What about you? Does Jesus Christ have your undivided loyalty, or do you maintain a very committed relationship with the kingdom of this world? Do you truly know whose side you are on, or are you trying to please both kingdoms at the same time? The Bible is unequivocal about this kind of duplicity. Friendship with the world is enmity with God. That should not hard to understand or difficult to believe. It would be like saying, in 1944, that friendship with the Nazis is enmity with the Allied forces. Of course it is! And that is how the Bible describes divided loyalties with the world. You cannot serve Jesus and serve the world. You cannot advance both causes. To whose cause do you belong? You cannot serve two masters. You cannot fight for opposing armies. And you cannot be neutral. Who is on the Lord's side?[121] Can you say that you are? Would Jesus say that you are?

The Allied invasion force also knew to expect extreme hardship. That doesn't mean that they enjoyed the hardship or made light of it. Far from it. But they knew to expect it. And they knew that they could not avoid or abandon the invasion effort because it was costly. What is your view of serving Christ and His kingdom? Do you accept hardship as a part of the effort? Do you expend more effort in your life trying to serve Christ or trying to achieve and maintain pleasant circumstances? Exactly how successful do you believe the Allied forces would have been if their main priority had been to avoid hardship rather than to accomplish their mission? Do you think that you will be successful for Christ if you place seeking your own comfort and pleasure above commitment to His cause?

Your viewpoint on this conflict—part of your "script"—makes all the difference in your living. If you see your life basically as your own, with religion as one of its components—important, certainly! by all means!—but just a part of your overall life; if much of your life is spent conforming to the world, trying to fit in without compromising, well… too much of your faith; if you love money or power or prestige more than you love Christ, no matter what you may say, but you try to add a little religion into this value system; if you think going to church basically "takes care of things," as far as religion is concerned; and if you think all this talk about two kingdoms with a war and the devil and sin and judgment is just a little too much on the extreme—maybe fanatical side; if this is your script or resembles your script, then my friend, I say to you in love and with respect that you have a faulty script. And what compounds your problem exponentially is that you think you are informed! Your false script of what it means to be a Christian is enabling you to live a life of self-deception. You may be in the condition of many of the Christians in Corinth, whom Paul said were in the flesh (as opposed to the Spirit) and could not understand spiritual matters. Or you may not be a Christian at all. God knows. But your script, if it resembles the statements above, no matter how comfortable you are with it, and no matter how many others seem to share it, is exactly that—*your* script. God is not obligated to honor your script.

God's word for you and for anyone else who belongs to Christ is that you are absolutely defined by your life in Him. You belong to Him. You are to seek His kingdom first. You are a child of God and friend of God and a servant of God. It does not mean that you are excessively "religious"—that your speech is filled with religious jargon and that you are constantly to be found at the place where a congregation meets. Does that sound even remotely like the life of Jesus? But what *does* sound like the life of Jesus is a life lived in absolute surrender to the will of the Father. A life of love and compassion but uncompromising in upholding truth and righteousness. A life of humility. A life of cross-bearing.[122] A life of joy and promise and healing and blessing. A life of faith and good works. A life filled with the Spirit of God, lived in the faithful use of His gifts. A life committed to destroying the strongholds of Satan, and setting people free who are in prisons of guilt, condemnation, brokenness, pain, and judgment. A life that clearly recognizes that there is evil in the world, that there is a kingdom of this world, that the devil rules that kingdom, and that the kingdom of God must advance in power and authority against spiritual forces of darkness. That is the life of Jesus, and if He has possession of you, that is your life—defined by God Himself.

What are you doing for God's kingdom? Do you know that there is a war on and that you are in it? Do you know whose side you are on, and do you have undivided loyalty to Christ? Are you prepared to suffer hardship for the kingdom of God?

Are you in the fight, or are you sitting in your tent? Or are you in denial about the whole thing? Is your life fruitful for God, or is your fruit being choked out by thorns and thistles of divided loyalty with the world?

Do you see yourself as a citizen of a definite kingdom, the kingdom of God, that is living and moving and acting with purpose within another kingdom, one that is alien and hostile to God and therefore to you, the kingdom of this world? Is this not only your concept but also a dominant concept? Do you understand that all of us who are of God's kingdom are sent into this hostile and fallen world in order to make disciples of Jesus Christ of all peoples? We are all, each one of us, including you, a part of God's rescue operation which is *the* theme of human history. Nothing in this world matters more for any person than whether or not he is reconciled to God, delivered from the world's kingdom, to become a citizen of the kingdom of God: saved from the judgment against sin, transformed into a new person by the power and gift of Christ. You, personally, are to have an *active role* in God's great work of salvation.

Jesus said that God knows you so well that even the hairs on your head are numbered. If God knows that, you can be assured that He knows what your spiritual gift is and that He desires you to use it. And when you begin to use your spiritual gift in God's service, you will be filled with joy and blessing as you see how God is pleased by your effort and uses you to contribute to the common good of His people, the Church.

Having said all of this, as important as our spiritual gifts and their uses are to the work of the kingdom and the health of the church, there is something else that is much more important to know. That is the subject of the next chapter.

Am I a soldier of the cross,
A follower of the Lamb?
And shall I fear to own His cause,
Or blush to speak His name?

Must I be carried to the skies
On flowery beds of ease,
While others fought to win the prize,
And sailed through bloody seas?

Are there no foes for me to face?
Must I not stem the flood?
Is this vile world a friend to grace,
To help me on to God?

Sure I must fight if I would reign;
Increase my courage, Lord!
I'll bear the toil, endure the pain,
Supported by thy Word.
                    —Isaac Watts

An All-Important
Interlude

By this all people will know that you are my disciples...
                                                    —John 13:35

The longest discussion of spiritual gifts in the New Testament is found in 1 Corinthians, chapters 12-14. But right in the middle of this teaching on spiritual gifts, there is a lengthy interruption. Paul breaks away in order to address what he calls "a more excellent way"—and this "more excellent way" is the love of God, or *agape. He* emphasizes that this love validates anything and everything we do—including the use of our spiritual gifts—and that a lack of agape invalidates anything we may do, even in God's name. Paul obviously felt that he should not continue writing about spiritual gifts until he had emphasized this much more important and overriding truth.

Paul's discussion of agape forms a chapter by itself, 1 Corinthians 13. It is one of the most quoted passages in the entire Bible, and it would be worthwhile here for us to review at least a part of this passage before we, like Paul's original hearers, go forward:

> If I speak in the tongues of men and of angels, but have not love, I am a noisy gong or a clanging cymbal. And if I have prophetic powers, and understand all mysteries and all knowledge, and if I have all faith, so as to remove mountains, but have not love, I am nothing. If I give away all I have, and if I deliver up my body to be burned, but have not love, I gain nothing.

> Love is patient and kind; love does not envy or boast; it is not arrogant or rude. It does not insist on its own way; it is not irritable or resentful; it does not rejoice at wrongdoing, but rejoices with the truth. Love bears all things, believes all things, hopes all things, endures all things.

Love never ends. ...So now faith, hope, and love abide, these three; but the greatest of these is love.

Paul reminds his hearers in poetical and unforgettable ways that exercising spiritual gifts is not the most important mark of our lives as Christians. Love is. The most important quality of the life of any person who knows God is the love of God. And in reminding his hearers of this truth, Paul echoes the teaching of Jesus Christ. When Jesus was asked what the greatest commandment was, He replied:

You shall love the Lord your God with all your heart and with all your soul and with all your mind. This is the great and first commandment. And a second is like it: You shall love your neighbor as yourself. On these two commandments depend all the Law and the Prophets.[123]

Jesus told us unequivocally what is most important to God: love. As we pause to make sure we understand this declaration of Jesus, we must not miss the astonishing summary He gave when He said that all of the Law and the Prophets depend on those two commandments. By the "Law and the Prophets," He meant everything the Bible teaches. Everything God requires of us. He taught that if we truly understand what it is to love God and to love our neighbor as ourselves we will be doing all that God requires. And this means, conversely, that failing to love, we cannot please God, no matter how gifted we are or busy we may be.

Jesus continued to reinforce the supremacy of *agape* throughout His ministry. When He knew that His departure was imminent, He told His disciples that "By this all people will know that you are my disciples, if you have love [*agape*] for one another."[124] Contrary to what we may sometimes seem to think, it is not by our organizations, or our buildings, or our power, or our influence that the world will recognize the disciples of Jesus—it is by our love, our agape. The apostle John said

Beloved, let us love one another, for love is from God, and whoever loves has been born of God and knows God. Anyone who does not love does not know God, because God is love.[125]

It is crucial for us to know that love, agape, is not a feeling. Love is the very character of God. It is the word that denotes God's selfless giving to all of His creation. And it represents the *relationship,* not the feelings, of Christ with us, His Church, His Bride.

If we do not have love, we are not only worthless to God's kingdom, we are a liability. Only to the degree that we love will the world take notice that we are of another realm. The devil will seek to persuade individuals or organizations to use his means for advancement and his substitutes for the love of Christ. And he will promise the world if we do so, just as he promised Jesus the world in his third temptation. But if we give into the devil's seduction and believe that love can be marginalized in favor of other attainments, we will be poor imitations of who God desires us to be. And we may be religious abominations. Failure to love is total failure.

The kingdom of God is where God reigns. And where God truly reigns there is love, His love, whether it is the heart of an individual, a marriage, a home, a family, a friendship, or a church. As the kingdom of God advances into this world, the message of that advance is the love of God and the character of that advance is the love of God in action. Without God's love, we *are* nothing and we *gain* nothing.

Gracious Spirit, Holy Ghost,
Taught by Thee we covet most
Of Thy gifts at Pentecost,
Holy, heavenly love.

Love is kind, and suffers long,
Love is meek, and thinks no wrong,
Love than death itself more strong;
Therefore, give us love.

Faith will vanish into sight;
Hope be emptied in delight;
Love in heaven will shine more bright;
Therefore, give us love.
—Christopher Wordsworth

THE CHURCH AND THE CHURCHES

In vain do they worship me, teaching as doctrines the commandments of men.

—Matthew 15:9

But the fruit of the Spirit is love, joy, peace, patience, kindness, goodness, faithfulness, gentleness, self-control; against such things there is no law.

—Galatians 5:22-23

What is the church, and how does being in the kingdom of God relate to belonging to a church? Must a Christian belong to a church? And if so, which church? Churches are quite different with extremely different beliefs and practices. They can't all be right! So which one is right? Or are all of them wrong? And if a Christian has to belong to a church, how active does he have to be? Should he attend every Sunday? Or just be regular, say once a month or so? Does he have to believe everything the church believes? In short, if I desire to belong to God's kingdom and serve Him with my spiritual gift, how do I make a decision about what church to go to, how often to go, and how much to invest myself in it?

The preceding paragraph is intentionally filled with the type of confusion that often accompanies a discussion about a person's proper relationship to church...or to churches. A major source of that confusion is that the word "church" is used to refer to different things in the same discussion, although the participants believe that they are talking about the same thing! Add to this problem that different parties attach their own particular beliefs, some deeply-held, some superficial, to the word *church* in all of its meanings, and you now have confusion that is greatly compounded.

So what is the Church? As we have already noted, the Greek word *ekklesia*, "church" means "called out ones." In the New Testament it means those who belong to Christ, those who have been called out of the kingdom of the world into the kingdom of God. Sometimes in the Scriptures "church" will be followed by the name of a particular place, such as the "church of God that is at Corinth" or by the name of the people who live in a particular place, such as the "church of the Thessalonians." But even in these more specific cases, it means the same thing—it means those who belong to Christ. Try substituting the phrase "heaven citizens" for "church." You can easily see how some teachings in the New Testament are about "heaven citizens" generally, and also how some letters might be addressed to the "heaven citizens" who are in Corinth or in Ephesus or Thessalonica. But in all of these cases, all of God's people, all of the "heaven citizens," whether generally or in a specific locale, are being identified.

Let's also look at what the word *church* never means in the Bible. It never means a building, as in "There sits my church." That would be like saying "There sits my heaven citizens." It never means a meeting, as in "I'm going to church." That, again, would be like saying "I'm going to heaven citizens."

The word *church* also never means "Eastside Baptist Church" in Corinth or the "First Avenue United Methodist Church of Corinth" or the "Greater Greece Assembly of God" or the "Corinth Independent Fundamental Church of the Bible" or the "Lutheran Church, Southern Greece Synod." It does not mean the Eastern Orthodox Church or Roman Catholic Church or Anglican or Reformed or Pentecostal or the "Faith Family Friendship Fellowship Church" or the "Hip Church at the Pointe." In the Bible, *church* does not mean a congregation or a denomination that is distinguishing itself from other congregations and denominations. It means God's people, and if a particular place is referenced, it means all of God's people in that place without even contemplating that the church in a certain place would be organized into separate camps. In fact, the closest reference to such a thing would be the situation in the Corinthian church where members were saying "I follow Paul," or "I follow Apollos," or "I follow Cephas," or "I follow Christ."[126] Paul's alarm at this division in the church was so profound that he opens his letter by addressing it at some length, roundly condemning such division, and appealing to the church to restore its unity. As Paul urged unity, he asked "Is Christ divided? Was Paul crucified for you? Or were you baptized in the name of Paul?"[127] These are rhetorical questions. Christ has not been divided. He was not divided then, and He is not divided now. Nor is His body divided. Jesus Christ died for us—not a congregation or denomination. And Christians are baptized in Christ's name, not in the name of a congregation or denomination.

So the Bible is clear and consistent in what is meant by the Church. It is clear and consistent in condemning division in the body of Christ. And it is clear and consistent in its teaching that Christ is the Head of His Church and that the Church is administered through the gifts and leading of the Holy Spirit. Nowhere does the Bible even suggest that Christ Himself would subordinate His role as the Head of the Church, or that the Holy Spirit would subordinate His role in gifting and leading its members to man-made organizational structures that may seek to impose themselves upon divine work—no matter how ancient and cultured or modern and popular those organizations may be.

Have you ever entered a foreign country for which you had to present your passport or returned home when you had to do the same? At busy border crossings there are different lines that persons enter, depending upon one's citizenship. For example, if you are entering a European country, there may be some lines for those with EU passports and different lines for those from other lands. On judgment day, there will not be different lines to heaven depending upon which church a person belonged to. There is no "Baptist" passport as opposed to a "Catholic" passport as opposed to an "Independent" passport. The only passport for God's kingdom of heaven is the one that is issued as a gift by Christ, and all who belong to Him carry the same passport.

So, are churches—meaning congregations and denominations—bad? Certainly not. More often than not, they are wonderful. Whether in their worship forms, ministry and mission endeavors, friendships, nurture of children, Christian education, family ministries, humanitarian enterprises, administration of the ordinances/sacraments, and cooperative endeavors—the good done by churches is immeasurable. When they are beacons for Christ and hospitals for sinners, when they proclaim a prophetic word to a lost world, when they seek to glorify their Lord and are led by Him in so doing, they are lights in the world's darkness.

But congregations and denominations are only partial and incomplete groupings within, or partially within, the true Church of Christ. A person, therefore, should not self-limit God's work in his life by believing and insisting that God can only use him within the structure of his particular congregation or denomination. Yes, God may choose to do so. But that is God's choice, not ours. Always be open to fellowship and cooperative ministry with Christians everywhere—within the Church of God—not just with your own particular congregation.

Congregations and denominations, like the people that populate them, are also flawed. A person should not expect a congregation or denomination to be perfect any more than one can expect his family members—even a spouse—to be perfect. No relationships are perfect—that includes church relationships. But unfortunately, even when making this allowance, we all recognize that some relationships can be so unhealthy—even abusive—that they must be rejected. And congregations and denominations can also deteriorate for many reasons (but with one basic cause—man's sin) to the point that those relationships must simply be abandoned for more healthy ones.

Only God Himself is worthy of our unqualified and absolute loyalty. If we give such loyalty to any other entity—including a congregation or denomination—we are giving the devil an opportunity for great harm. Throughout the ages, some congregations and denominations have been used by the devil for hell's purposes, inflicting pain and destruction upon individuals, towns, cities, and nations, blaspheming the very name of Christ. And they continue to be so used today when ungodly people take control and the gullible or weak follow them with blind loyalty.

We see this abuse easily and comfortably when we look at history—especially the history of others! In Europe, the centuries are awash in the blood of helpless Christians tortured and killed, not by pagans, but by other so-called Christians, not over any crimes committed but over various theological views—all this done in the name of the Church, in the name of Christ! How many wars have been fought under Christian vs. Christian flags? Some European churches in their lust for power have been greatly compromised by entanglement with governments, including some hellish ones, right up through the Nazi era. Some might say until our own era.

We find these things somewhat easy to see and to condemn when we are protected by time or distance—and when it is not us! But we do not find such offenses as easy to see and condemn when they are closer to home. We must often be reminded that religious persecution did not cease and desist when America was colonized. Ask some Quakers who were tarred and feathered or preachers from "unauthorized" denominations in various American colonies who were fined and imprisoned for preaching without a license. There are reasons that the Bill of Rights was both fought for and controversial when our Constitution was ratified. And throughout our own history in America, many churches and people in those churches have supported whatever the prevailing political and economic spirits seems to suggest: slavery, child labor, racism, and ethnic hate—or remained silent in the face of it. Churches have often served and continue to serve as power bases for complete worldlings in their cities or communities, and many churches today are places where religious platitudes can be freely proclaimed but where the true, prophetic word of God spoken to those who need to hear it would get a minister fired immediately, or worse.

So, should you identify with a congregation or denomination? Yes, in general, you should. Identify with a Christian community—one where Christ is honored in the living out of the gospel as well as where sound preaching and teaching may be found. Go where the love of Christ is paramount. Go where God leads you. Don't expect perfection, and don't forget that you are not perfect. Do not forget that your congregation or denomination is not *the* Church—no matter what anyone says. Always seek God's kingdom first—and if you do not, if you develop a stronger loyalty to your congregation or denomination than you have to the Lord Jesus Himself, be assured that the devil will exploit it. Imperfections allowed for, do not hesitate to leave a congregation or denomination, if the devil has so gained control that your involvement there is actually a painful impediment to your ability to live for Christ. But Jesus has called us to live in community, and it appears that until He returns, His Church will be divided by countless groupings. So identify with a church somewhere, but do not lose perspective.

One sign of losing perspective is when you begin to identify far more with your congregation or denomination than you do with being a citizen of the kingdom of God, a person who is called out of the world to belong exclusively to Jesus Christ. Membership in Christ's one body is the membership that matters the most—and by far! That is the communion that is true and eternal. Because a congregation or denominations can become almost hopelessly entangled with the unsaved world in more ways than can possibly be addressed here, it is often possible for a person to be a shallow, worldly, compromised Christian and still be a "outstanding member of the [fill in the blank] church." If your primary source of Christian identity—your script—is, more than anything else, to be a good member of such and such a church or denomination, you may not able to follow Christ in single-minded commitment and devotion because of conflicted and confused loyalties. Loyalty to Christ must always trump loyalty to an institution or anyone in it.

Every description, every teaching of who we are as God's people emphasizes that we are called out from the masses of people who do not know God to be a unique people who belong to Him heart, body, and soul. God's people are referred to as His chosen people. We are told to be separate from the world, that we are holy to the Lord, that we are the Bride of Christ, God's own possession. We are told not to be conformed to the world but to be transformed by the renewing of our minds, to lay aside our old natures, to walk in the Spirit. Jesus said that no one who puts his hand to the plow and looks back is fit for the kingdom of God.

Now let me ask you something? Would this be the fair and common description of the members of American congregations or denominations? Are the members of our churches known for their holy living and their refusal to compromise devotion to Christ for any worldly attainment? In their everyday living, are they fairly perceived as being different from those who do not know Christ? How about you? Do others say of you that you are not like everyone else? Do you demonstrate in your living that you are called out of the world? That you are distinctly different with different values and loyalties? Do you have a different life within and without that points to your Lord Jesus Christ? Or have you made yourself feel better about living a shallow life for Christ because you receive affirmation and kudos at your "church" every week? You're a good "church member" or a good [fill in the blank with the name of your denomination].

It may seem that my view of congregations and denominations is a negative one. That is not the case. I praise God for churches and have spent my life in them. Congregations and denominations are, many of them, used greatly by God for His kingdom, and they are filled with many people who love God, love others, and serve God faithfully. They seek to honor God and be a loving community of faith. But none of them is "the" Church, none should receive our blind devotion, none should become an idol that we worship and serve in place of Christ. Being loyal to Christ first and foremost and seeking His kingdom first will make you the best church member you can possibly be, although everyone in a church may not always see you that way.

Jesus did not give blind unqualified loyalty to religious institutions, teachings, and traditions. He did support them in their appropriate roles and participated in them, while standing for truth and living with uncompromised integrity. Let Him be your pattern.

Christ is made the sure foundation,
*   Christ the Head and Corner-stone,*
Chosen of the Lord, and precious,
*   Binding all the Church in one,*
Holy Sion's help for ever,
*   And her confidence alone.*
                    —Latin hymn, trans. J. M Neale

FINAL THINGS

If you abide in my word, you are truly my disciples, and you will know the truth, and the truth will set you free.

—John 8:31-32

Ask almost anyone in a church, or even anyone off the street to complete this phrase, "You shall know the truth…," and a great number of them will say, "and the truth will set you free." The phrase has become proverbial. You will even see it as a slogan in many a newspaper banner—not just religious ones. Ask the same people if they know who said it, and the church folks generally *will* know while those who are not church folks may not. Then ask all the same people if they can quote the first part of Jesus' statement, and the numbers will not only drop dramatically, they will be at near zero among both groups. This phrase, "You shall know the truth, and the truth shall set you free" may be one of the most out-of-context and, therefore, misrepresented phrases often quoted in the English language.

Jesus made this statement in the midst of what was actually a rather adversarial discussion with religious people, some who were believing in Him and others who definitely were not. This particular statement was made to those who were believing. It is a conditional statement, an if-then proposition. He told them if—if—they abide in His word—then—they are truly His disciples—and, then, and only then—they would know the truth, which would set them free.

Abiding in Jesus' word means more than reading your Bible every day. Throughout many centuries, most Christians did not even have Bibles, or any other books for that matter. And they couldn't have read a book if they had owned one. And today, in many parts of the world, owning a Bible and reading it daily is not an option. But it probably *is* an option for you. So let me ask you: do you read your Bible daily? If not, why don't you? Do you watch TV daily? Do you have conversations with others daily? Do you listen to music or to talk radio daily? Do you read the newspaper daily? Do you work out daily or enjoy hobbies daily? Why don't you read your Bible daily? Are you too busy? Are you so busy you don't have 10 minutes for the Bible? Or five minutes? That is busy!

Are you a disciple of Jesus? I don't mean are you a "Christian" according to some convenient script you may have come up with. Are you a disciple of Jesus? And if you are, as a disciple of Jesus, do you believe that a daily time of Bible reading is important? Or do you get all you need in church once a week? Or once in a while? Is that what Jesus taught about discipleship?

If you belong to Jesus Christ, if you are a disciple, you need a time of private prayer and Bible reading every day. Is this legalism? If someone tells you that you should drink water every day, is that legalism? If you are told to eat every day, is that legalism? If you are told to give time to important relationships every day, is that legalism? If you are told you need daily exercise, is that legalism? If you desire to be a true disciple of Jesus, being told to abide in His word, and that this generally includes daily prayer and Bible reading, is not legalism. It is help! It is guidance in being a disciple!

Following Christ is not a philosophy. It is not an ethical system. And it sure isn't a mere statement of theological propositions that you agree are true. Following Jesus is your very life given over to Him. He is the center of your universe. And His word is your nourishment. It is inspired by Him and blessed by Him. Time spent with Jesus in prayer and in His word is the most precious time of your day. And Jesus Himself has told us that to be His true disciples we are to abide, to continue in, to dwell in His word. This is not for religious "fanatics." This is for Christians, and if you belong to Christ, it is for you. Jesus said

> If anyone loves me, he will keep my word, and my Father will love him, and we will come to him and make our home with him. Whoever does not

love me does not keep my words. And the word that you hear is not mine but the Father's who sent me.[128]

If we abide in His word, we are true disciples. How can that be? Doesn't following Christ consist of more than reading the Bible. Certainly. But those who abide in the word of Christ, those who spend time with Him and His word, will be changed by that word. The word of God is living and active. Through His word God will speak to your deepest needs, and His word, blessed by His Spirit, becomes a catalyst in your life for transformation. As we spend time, reverently and humbly, in His word, we are taught and blessed and directed and molded into the image of our Lord and Teacher. We become doers of the word owing in large measure to the regular time we spend in the word. As the Apostle James wrote "the one who looks into the perfect law, the law of liberty, and perseveres, being no hearer who forgets but a doer who acts, he will be blessed in his doing.[129]

When you spend time in God's word, you will be amazed at how often the challenges you face each day will have been addressed in your Scripture reading that very morning. You will find some behaviors checked by God's word and other behaviors encouraged as you go through the day. You will be empowered with the promises of God, and you will learn to depend on those promises with faith when times are tough.

All Christians need help in understanding more and more fully what God's word means, how to understand especially some of the more difficult parts of Scripture, and how to apply it to their living. And the Holy Spirit supplies preachers and teachers in the Church to help us in just that way. Nearly unlimited resources exist to help us in our Bible study and Christian living. But there is no substitute for a daily, personal time, devoted to God, spent in prayer and Bible study, in which we allow Him to speak to us through His word and His word to be implanted into our lives.

For centuries, Church authorities tried, with great success actually, to keep the Bible even from being translated into the language of the people. Courageous men, some of them martyred and all of them persecuted, broke through these restraints and dared to translate the

Scriptures into common languages. Such Bibles were banned, and owning one was punishable by death. But the word of God could not be restrained. Eventually governments, both secular and religious, were forced to allow, even authorize, Bibles in the common languages of the day. Bibles are still banned in lands where it is feared. But in our land and many others, because of the courage and spilled blood of the martyrs, all of us are able to own Bibles in our language and read them without fear of persecution or death for so doing. One can only imagine what this company of martyrs must think as they look on and see our Bibles collecting dust, buried under a stack of magazines somewhere, while we serve the gods of comfort and convenience and ease and call it all Christianity.

Some Christians and so-called Christians simply have no interest in God's word, but others truly have tried to cultivate this daily habit and failed every time. The reason is that Christians are opposed in this effort by the ruler of this world, the devil, and all his evil forces. No, he does not appear in a red suit sporting a pitchfork and tell you not to read your Bible. But if you are one who has tried to cultivate this habit before and failed, have you noticed when you head for the Bible and your place of prayer how suddenly your mind will be seized with one or two urgent things you had better take care of first? Or how the phone will ring? Or a text message will arrive that needs an answer right now? Have you noticed how you just can't seem to get up early enough to have this time and how at night, no matter what time you choose, once you begin to read your Bible you immediately get so sleepy? The devil does not want you to abide in God's word—be assured of that. He fears the word of God. He knows its power. And he will oppose you in this effort.

So what can you do? It's simple, but you will not want to do it. Confess to God that you are not adequate in your own strength to cultivate this habit, confess that He must help you or you will fail, and ask Him to work in you and with you to give you the victory. You will not want to make this confession because of your pride. You can do it yourself! You don't need a crutch! So let me ask you, are you being successful? The devil is far more knowledgeable that you are. He is a far greater intelligence, and compared to his power you have none. Your victory is not in your own strength. It is in Christ, your Helper, whose Spirit dwells in you. Greater is He that is in you than he that is in the world.[130] And when you mortify your pride, confess your weakness, and ask for His help, you will receive it. You may stumble some along the way, but you will not fail. As you look to your Lord in faith, He will give you the victory.[131]

Seek first the kingdom of God. Live as a joyful, liberated citizen of the eternal kingdom of God. Live for Christ, and let Him live through you. Joyfully exercise your spiritual gift. Abide in His word, allowing Him to do the work in your life which He has planned from all eternity. If you do this, you will know the truth, and the truth will set you free.

Father, for Your light I pray:
  A wisdom from above,
A unity of mind with You,
  A walk of faith and love;

A confidence in every step,
  A singleness of will,
A clarity of word and deed,
  Anxiety made still.
                                    —W.B.

ENDNOTES

1 Matthew 4:1
2 Matthew 4:8-10
3 1 John 3:8
4 John 8:44
5 Matthew 13:37-39
6 Luke 8:11-12
7 John 12:31 (emphasis mine)
8 John 14:30-31 (emphasis mine)
9 John 16:11 (emphasis mine)
10 Hebrews 2:14
11 Ephesians 6:11-12
12 1 Corinthians 15:24
13 1 Peter 5:8
14 Revelation 2:10
15 Revelation 12:9
16 John 17:6
17 John 17:9
18 John 17:14-16
19 John 17:25
20 Acts 19:8 (emphasis mine)
21 Acts 20:25 (emphasis mine)
22 Acts 28:30-31 (emphasis mine)
23 1 Corinthians 2:12 (emphasis mine)
24 1 Corinthians 11:32 (emphasis mine)
25 Colossians 2:8 (emphasis mine)
26 James 4:4
27 2 Peter 1:4
28 1 John 2:15-17
29 1 John 4:4-6
30 Rev. 11:15

31 Paul often referred to himself as a bondservant, a slave, of Jesus Christ, and in the Bible, followers of Christ are often referred to as bondservants. While those who are in Christ have been elevated from the level of servant to that of friend and child, the state of servanthood is always present in our lives—unto God and one another.

32 Any number of present-day constitutional monarchies have sovereigns who are held in high regard by their subjects. But these royals, as we all know, do not wield the absolute authority of the kings of old. There are, perhaps, some present-day kings with great, if not absolute, authority, but these may not generally be held in as high a regard or serve as particularly good examples of a "good" king.

33 1 Corinthians 15:28
34 Matthew 4:17
35 Matthew 6:33
36 Matthew 18:3

[37] Luke 13:25-29
[38] John 15:16; 3:7
[39] 2 Corinthians 5:19-20
[40] Matthew 11:28
[41] Revelation 22:17
[42] 2 Peter 3:9
[43] Luke 12:32
[44] Hebrews 3:12-15
[45] Matthew 25:41
[46] Matthew 10:33
[47] Mark 9:47-48
[48] 2 Timothy 2:12
[49] Revelation 20:15
[50] Matthew 13:20-21
[51] Luke 9:62
[52] Revelation 2:10, emphasis mine
[53] 2 Timothy 2:11-13
[54] John 1:11-12
[55] John 3:16
[56] John 14:6
[57] John 17:14-16
[58] Matthew 5:14
[59] Matthew 5:13
[60] 2 Corinthians 5:17
[61] Romans 8:9
[62] Galatians 3:2-3
[63] Romans 8:9
[64] Acts 19:1-2
[65] Ephesians 1:13-14
[66] James 2:19
[67] Galatians 5:22-23
[68] 2 Peter 3:18
[69] Luke 23:43
[70] John 3:3
[71] called the "rapture" in some Christian circles
[72] Hebrews 12:22-24
[73] Revelation 6:14
[74] 2 Timothy 4:8
[75] 2 Thessalonians 1:7-10
[76] Matthew 25:34
[77] Matthew 25:41
[78] Matthew 25:46
[79] 2 Peter 3:10-13
[80] Revelation 21:1
[81] Revelation 21:3-4
[82] Revelation 21:6-8
[83] Acts 4:12
[84] Luke 17:20-21
[85] Romans 14:17
[86] 1 Corinthians 4:20

[87] "Christ" is Greek for "Messiah"

[88] Romans 14:1

[89] Romans 14:18-19

[90] Matthew 28:18-20

[91] This is certainly not to suggest that the Lord never sends people to specific places. Of course He does. And missions was originated by the Holy Spirit Himself. But the Great Commission is for all believers, going forward in Christ's name and service, wherever they are.

[92] 1 Thessalonians 5:11

[93] Matthew 3:7-8

[94] 1 John 3:7-10

[95] John 16:8

[96] John 16:14

[97] Galatians 5:19-21

[98] Galatians 5:19-21 (from J. B. Phillips, *The New Testament in Modern English*, 1962 edition by HarperCollins)

[99] Galatians 5:22-23

[100] Mark 12:28-34

[101] Hosea 6:6

[102] Matthew 9:13

[103] Matthew 12:7-8

[104] John 3:8

[105] Acts 10:38

[106] John 4:24

[107] 1 Corinthians 12:7-12

[108] here and elsewhere, "gift" to mean a gift *or gifts*—some Christians have more than one

[109] 1 Corinthians 12:27

[110] "Some" does not mean "all." If these problems do not exist in your particular church, that is wonderful. May your tribe increase.

[111] 1 Corinthians 6:19-20

[112] Ephesians 5:17; 1 Thessalonians 4:13

[113] Romans 12:4-8

[114] 1 Corinthians 12:4-6

[115] 1 Corinthians 2:3-4

[116] Mark 3:17

[117] 1 Corinthians 3:1-3

[118] James 1:5-8

[119] Galatians 1:10

[120] Matthew 6:4

[121] Exodus 32:26

[122] Matthew 10:38;16:24; Mark 8:34; Luke 9:23;14:27

[123] Matthew 22:37-40

[124] John 13:35

[125] 1 John 4:7-8

[126] 1 Corinthians 1:12

[127] 1 Corinthians 1:13

[128] John 14:23-24

[129] James 1:25

[130] 1 John 4:4

[131] 1 John 5:4

For more information or for spiritual encouragement, contact

ChristLife Ministries
P O Box 8043
Huntsville, TX 77340
www.theChristLife.org

or you can email Wayne Barrett at

ChristLife@suddenlink.net

And I am sure of this, that he who began a good work in you will bring it to completion at the day of Jesus Christ.
—Philippians1:6

Made in the USA
Middletown, DE
04 October 2017